Brilliant Office Microsoft®
2010 for the Over 50s

Joli Ballew

Prentice Hall
an imprint of

PEARSON

Harlow, England • London • New York • Boston • San Francisco • Toronto • Sydney • Singapore • Hong Kong
Tokyo • Seoul • Taipei • New Delhi • Cape Town • Madrid • Mexico City • Amsterdam • Munich • Paris • Milan

Pearson Education Limited
Edinburgh Gate
Harlow CM20 2JE
United Kingdom
Tel: +44 (0)1279 623623
Fax: +44 (0)1279 431059
Website: www.pearsoned.co.uk

First published in Great Britain in 2011

The rights of Joli Ballew to be identified as authors of this work have been asserted
by her in accordance with the Copyright, Designs and Patents Act 1988.

Pearson Education is not responsible for the content of third party internet sites.

ISBN: 978-0-273-74572-3

British Library Cataloguing-in-Publication Data
A catalogue record for this book is available from the British Library

Library of Congress Cataloging-in-Publication Data
Ballew, Joli.
   Brilliant Microsoft Office 2010 for the over 50s / Joli Ballew.
      p. cm. -- (Brilliant guides)
   ISBN 978-0-273-74572-3 (pbk.)
 1.   Microsoft Office. 2.   Business--Computer programs. I. Title.
   HF5548.4.M525B353 2011
   005.5--dc22

                                              2010050500

Microsoft product screenshots reprinted with permission from Microsoft
Corporation.

10 9 8 7 6 5 4 3 2 1
15 14 13 12 11

Typeset in 11pt Arial Condensed by 30
Printed and bound by Rotolito Lombarda, Italy

Brilliant guides

What you need to know and how to do it

When you're working on your computer and come up against a problem that you're unsure how to solve, or want to accomplish something in an application that you aren't sure how to do, where do you look? Manuals and traditional training guides are usually too big and unwieldy and are intended to be used as end-to-end training resources, making it hard to get to the info you need right away without having to wade through pages of background information that you just don't need at that moment – and helplines are rarely that helpful!

Brilliant guides have been developed to allow you to find the info you need easily and without fuss and guide you through the task using a highly visual, step-by-step approach – providing exactly what you need to know when you need it!

Brilliant guides provide the quick easy-to-access information that you need, using a table of contents and troubleshooting guide to help you find exactly what you need to know, and then presenting each task in a visual manner. Numbered steps guide you through each task or problem, using numerous screenshots to illustrate each step. Added features include 'See also...' boxes that point you to related tasks and information in the book, while 'Did you know?...' sections alert you to relevant expert tips, tricks and advice to further expand your skills and knowledge.

In addition to covering all major office PC applications, and related computing subjects, the *Brilliant* series also contains titles that will help you in every aspect of your working life, such as writing the perfect CV, answering the toughest interview questions and moving on in your career.

Brilliant guides are the light at the end of the tunnel when you are faced with any minor or major task.

Acknowledgements

I am so thankful for the opportunities the people at Pearson have given me; I've written over a dozen books in the Brilliant and In Simple Steps series, and they continue to come back to me for more. Steve Temblett, Katy Robinson and the rest of the crew are fantastic to work with and they give me free rein over content and voice, and are encouraging at every turn.

I am particularly fond of the books in the 'Over 50's' series. My readers are loyal, enthusiastic and ready to learn, and as I always suggest, they contact me when they're in trouble. Should you, dear reader, ever need a bit of encouragement or a solution to a simple computer problem, feel free to contact me at joli_ballew@hotmail.com. I answer all email, and I'd love to hear from you.

I would like to acknowledge my family too: Dad, Cosmo, Jennifer and Andrew, and my extended family, Garth, Theresa, Doug, Laura and Nathan. Hopefully, in a couple of years we'll have more names in this list by way of more grandchildren!

I also have a close relationship with my agent, Neil Salkind of the Salkind Literary Agency. I'd like to send a big thanks to Neil, since this year will be our tenth year of working together. We've managed to get close to 50 books published in that time, which is no small feat for author or agent. He has other clients, and I know that, but he keeps me busy and keeps me writing, and is always there with a smile and a helping hand. I doubt an author in my field can often say that they have 'too much' work, and on occasion, I have to say that to Neil. It's nice to continue to earn my income from writing, especially when I can do it at home and at my leisure. Thanks, Neil, I couldn't do it without you.

Finally, I have quite a few very dear friends that think I'm some sort of genius, even though I'm not. Just because I know a lot about computers doesn't mean I can spout off Pi to 30 digits, tell you which way is north from where I'm standing, or what time it is in New York. I'm just plugging along like everyone else, working to make the world a better (and more knowledgeable) place.

Dedication

For Neil Salkind, my agent and friend; it's been a great ten years.

About the author

Joli Ballew is an award-winning, best-selling, technical author of 40+ books. Joli has been working with computers, gadgets and all things media since her freshman year in college in 1982, where even then, she was aware of her interests and majored in Computer Science (with a minor in English Literature). Joli has served as a technical editor for various books, and is currently the series editor for Pearson Education's In Simple Steps series. Joli has written over a dozen books for Pearson in the past few years herself. Additionally, Joli has written over 400 articles for Brighthub.com, and created, manages and posts daily to her Facebook Group How to Do Everything: iPad. Joli is a Microsoft MVP and holds several Microsoft certifications. In her free time, Joli enjoys working out at her local gym, gardening, playing with her two cats, Pico and Lucy, and pottering around the house.

Contents

Getting started with Microsoft Office 2010

Introduction

Microsoft Office 2010 is one of the newest additions to the Microsoft family. If you've used a computer in a work environment in the last 15 or so years, chances are you've had experience with some earlier incarnation of it. You may have used Office 95, Office 97, Office 2000, Office 2003, or another version, and may already know how to perform some tasks. Microsoft Office 2010 outdoes each of these previous versions, though, and offers more than a few new features you'll wonder how you ever lived without.

If you're familiar with Microsoft's earlier Office applications (excluding Office 2007), you're going to be quite surprised by the *Ribbon*. (If you've never used Microsoft Office you won't have to *unlearn* anything because the Ribbon won't be the cause of any learning curve!) The old tabs that previously contained drop-down menus are gone, replaced by tabs that contain groups of commands. These groups contain commands that logically go together; for instance, on Word's Insert tab there's a group named Illustrations, where you'll find commands for inserting a picture, clip art, a shape, SmartArt and charts.

The commands in a tab's groups are often represented by icons too. These icons make finding what you want easier and faster than browsing through a long list of commands in a drop-down menu. Icons are simply easier on our over-50 eyes. The icons you'll find on the Ribbon for each application (Word, Excel, Outlook and PowerPoint) are not unique to the program either. For instance, the icon for inserting a picture is the same for every application and is under the same tab, so once you know how to insert a picture in Word, you can easily insert a picture in other applications using the same method.

In this chapter you'll learn about some of the similarities among the various Office applications. You'll learn about the Ribbon, command groups, and start to recognise the commands you'll see in almost all Office applications. You'll learn how to navigate the File tab, create Desktop shortcuts to applications so you can access them more quickly, and how to change options related to Office programs (such as the colour of the interface or the items on the Quick Access toolbar).

?

Did you know?

The top left corner of any Office window offers a small icon to designate the program you're using. Look for the blue W in the figure here, just above the File tab.

Microsoft Office is a productivity suite of applications. Millions of people all over the world use Microsoft Office to create, manage and edit presentations, data, databases, documents and publications, and to manage their email. Microsoft Office is not included with any Microsoft operating system (such as Windows XP, Windows Vista or Windows 7); you have to purchase Microsoft Office separately. It's perfectly fine to install and run Office 2010 on any of these computers though. Office 2010 will run just fine on an older Office XP machine, too (in case your kids have retired a computer to you!).

There are a dozen Office applications to choose from, and they are organised for purchase into various collections called suites. While a corporation may need a suite that contains programs you're probably unfamiliar with, such as SharePoint Workspace, InfoPath or Access, the suite you've purchased likely has more consumer-friendly and familiar applications such as Word, Excel, PowerPoint and Outlook.

The five most popular Microsoft Office suites available to the average consumer are:

- Office Home and Business 2010 – Word, Excel, PowerPoint, Outlook, OneNote, 90 days of technical support.
- Office Home and Student 2010 – Word, Excel, PowerPoint, OneNote, 90 days of technical support.
- Office Professional 2010 – Word, Excel, PowerPoint, Outlook, OneNote, Publisher, Access, one year of technical support.
- Office Professional Academic 2010 – Word, Excel, PowerPoint, Outlook, OneNote, Publisher, Access, 90 days of technical support.
- Office Mobile 2010 – Word, Excel, PowerPoint, Outlook, OneNote.

In this book we'll cover the most common applications: Word, Excel, Outlook and PowerPoint.

What is Microsoft Office?

1

Jargon buster

Microsoft Office is an *application*, while Windows XP, Windows Vista and Windows 7 are *operating systems*.

Important

A new computer may come with a trial version of Microsoft Office installed, but you still have to pay for the program when the trial is up (or purchase and install it yourself if no trial is included).

What is Microsoft Office? (cont.)

Learn more about Microsoft Office Suites

1. Connect to the Internet and visit www.office.microsoft.com

2. Look for a link that says 'Compare Suites' or something similar.

3. Note what programs are included in each suite.

Did you know?

If you decide you'd like to add a program to your Microsoft suite, for instance, Publisher, you can purchase the stand-alone program from Microsoft.

Timesaver tip

Use Word to create letters to insurance companies or doctors, flyers for a lost dog or a community event, or to manage simple lists of data in tables.

Word

You'll use Word to create documents. A document may be a simple letter or a quick note you need to print and fax, or it can be much more. You can use Word to create a flyer or publication, to manage a group of data, or even write your first novel, complete with a Table of Contents, headers and footers.

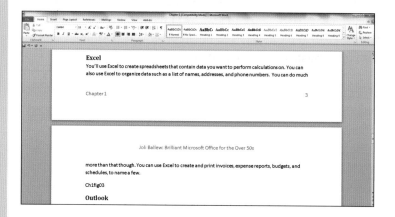

Excel

You'll use Excel to create spreadsheets that contain data on which you want to perform calculations. You can also use Excel to organise data such as a list of names, addresses and phone numbers (although Word may be easier for this). You can do much more than that, though; you can use Excel to create and print invoices, expense reports, budgets and schedules, to name a few.

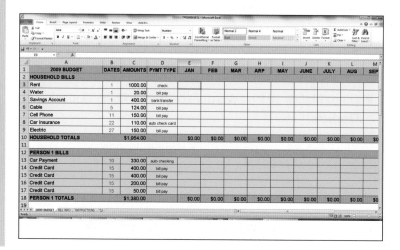

Outlook

Outlook is an email management application. You'll do the usual with it, including sending and receiving email, but you can also manage the email you want to keep by organising the data in folders and subfolders. You can create rules for incoming mail. You can even delay the delivery of emails you want to send. Here you can see the Outlook interface and the composition of an email in progress. The tabs in Outlook and the tabs available in an email differ.

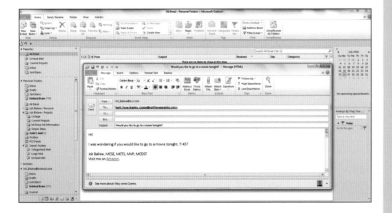

PowerPoint

PowerPoint is the application you'll use for creating slideshows and presentations. You can create and show presentations at retirement parties, business kiosks, or even for your own pleasure, perhaps to organise photos from a recent holiday. You can even use PowerPoint to create invitations.

Timesaver tip

Use Excel to manage your household budget or the budget for a golf league or community centre, and to create invoices, expense reports, health logs and any other document that requires calculations be performed on the data.

Did you know?

When creating email, note that you can insert pictures and edit them, and even attach music and video.

What is Microsoft Office? (cont.)

Learn more about a specific application

1. Connect to the Internet and visit www.office.microsoft.com

2. Click the name of the program you'd like to know more about.

3. Click Watch the Demo, Office 2010 Support, Get Started with <program name> 2010, and other links.

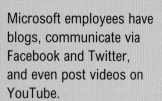

See also

Microsoft employees have blogs, communicate via Facebook and Twitter, and even post videos on YouTube.

Timesaver tip

Use PowerPoint to create multi-slide presentations but also to create one-slide files like award certificates, calendars, greeting cards and invitations.

OneNote

Your suite of applications likely also includes OneNote; all but the Office Starter 2010 do. OneNote enables you to gather information from various sources (including audio, text and the Web) and organise that data effectively. People often use OneNote on a Tablet PC because OneNote can transcribe written text into typed text, which is a great feature for college students and those that attend meetings and conferences often. If you have trouble typing but can write with a pen okay, you may prefer a Tablet PC and OneNote over Word. You can also use OneNote to collaborate with others. If you are interested in learning more, check out www.office.microsoft.com/onenote

You have to locate the programs for Microsoft Office to open them. They may be on your Desktop, on the Taskbar, and/or on the Start menu. If you're unsure about what areas of your computer we're talking about, we've included a tutorial. Once you've found the icon or shortcut to the program, simply click it (or double-click it) to open it.

Desktop

The Desktop is the part of your screen that you see when no programs or windows are open. It's the part of the screen that holds the background image and Desktop icons. You may already have shortcuts to your Office programs here.

Taskbar

The Taskbar is the bar that runs (almost always) across the bottom of the screen, although it can be moved to the sides or the top. A taskbar can be configured in many ways, including with its icons grouped or ungrouped. When a program is open, the related icon appears here. Note that in this figure Outlook, Word and Excel are open; PowerPoint is not. In this instance, PowerPoint is 'pinned' to the Taskbar.

Note: The section on the right side of the Taskbar is called the Notification Area or the System Tray.

Start any Microsoft Office application

1

! Important

These screenshots are from a Windows 7 PC. While the Desktop, Taskbar and Start Menu are located in the same place and function in the same manner on Windows XP and Windows Vista computers, their components will not look exactly like what you see here.

See also

In the next section you'll learn how to create shortcuts on the Desktop.

For your information

You can also make changes to the Start Menu from the Start Menu tab.

Start any Microsoft Office application (cont.)

Configure the Taskbar

1. Right-click the Taskbar.
2. Click Properties.
3. Explore the settings. Consider deselecting Use Small Icons.
4. Make other changes as desired.
5. Click OK.

Create a shortcut to an application

1. Click the Start button or the Start orb.
2. Click Programs or All Programs.
3. Click Microsoft Office.
4. Right-click the program for which you want to create a shortcut.
5. Click Send to. Click Desktop (Create Shortcut). (Depending on the options available to you, you may be able to 'pin' a shortcut to the Start menu or the Taskbar. When you pin a program an icon appears in there until you 'unpin' it.)
6. Repeat as desired.

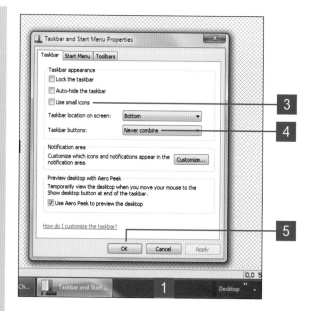

Start menu

The Start menu is accessed by clicking the Start button or Start orb in the bottom left corner, in the farthest left position on the Taskbar. From there, click Programs or All Programs to view all of the programs installed on your computer, and to locate the Microsoft Office folder and installed applications. You'll have to get here to create shortcuts for the programs you'll use often.

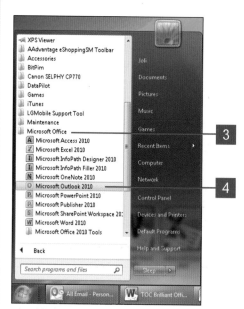

When you first open any of the four programs we'll cover in this book – Word, Excel, Outlook or PowerPoint – you'll notice the Ribbon and its tabs. The items that appear in the Ribbon change when you move from tab to tab. So, what you see when you click the Home tab is different from what you see when you click the Insert tab, the Page Layout tab, the Review tab, and so on.

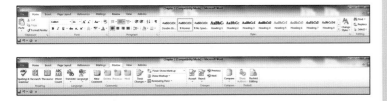

No matter what version of the Ribbon you're viewing though, there are Command Groups available. The groups are named, as you can see here. In the second screenshot, the Review tab has groups for Proofing, Language, Comments, Tracking, Changes, Compare and Protect. In some instances a command in a Command Group will include a down arrow that offers additional options.

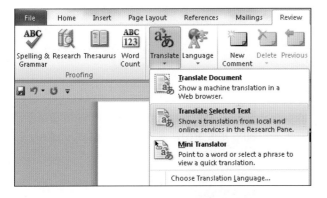

In other instances, a group may offer a down-facing arrow beside the group name. You can click this arrow to see additional options. One place you'll find this feature is the Home tab in Word, Excel and PowerPoint in the Font group (or under the Message tab in Outlook in a new email in the Basic Text group). Clicking the arrow in the Font group opens an entirely new window of features, called a dialogue box. If you find that the Font dialogue box is easier to use than

Explore the Ribbon and tabs (cont.)

the Ribbon, feel free to use it. It includes the same options available in the Font group as well as additional options.

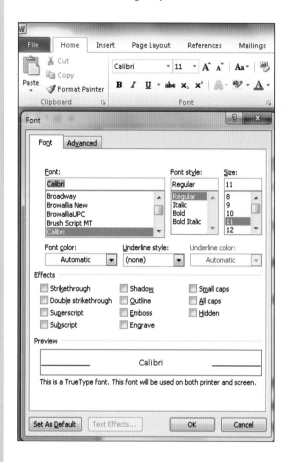

Timesaver tip

Sometimes, clicking the downward arrow in a group causes a sidebar to appear.

In another instance, a particular section in a command group offers an arrow. Clicking this arrow almost always opens additional options that can be applied using the command. For instance, in PowerPoint, from the Design tab and the Themes group, you can access several themes from the Ribbon. There are others available, though, as you can discern from the down-facing arrow in Themes. Click the arrow to access all of the available options for the group.

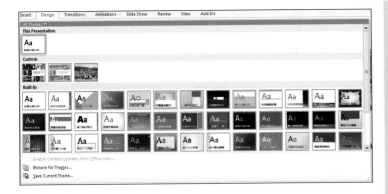

Finally, sometimes new tabs appear! This happens when you click a picture, a chart, a table, or other element in a file you're creating or editing. When a new tab appears, there are even more options from the Ribbon. (Sometimes, two tabs appear!) Here are a couple of examples: the two Video Tools tabs appear when a video is selected inside a PowerPoint slide; the Picture Tools tab appears when a picture is selected inside a new email in Outlook.

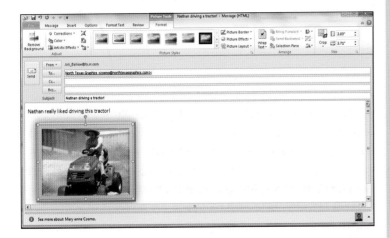

Explore the Ribbon and tabs

1 Open Microsoft Office Word.

2 The Home tab is selected by default. Notice the Command Groups:

   a Clipboard

   b Font

   c Paragraph

   d Styles

   e Editing.

3 Click the Insert tab. Notice the Command Groups:

   f Pages

   g Tables

   h Illustrations

   i Links

   j Header & Footer

   k Text

   l Symbols.

4 Repeat with the remaining tabs (excluding the File tab).

5 Repeat with Excel and PowerPoint.

Important

If you've already set up Outlook, explore it too. Otherwise, save this exploration for later.

Understand the File tab

Each of the Office programs we'll cover in this book has a File tab. The File tab stands apart from the other tabs because instead of offering the (by now) familiar Ribbon, it offers *more tabs* that are positioned vertically. These tabs offer options such as Save, Print, New and the like. These are the same options you're used to seeing under the original File tab of older Office programs, but they've been given a different look. Most of the Office programs you'll be using will have the options you see here, including Save, Save As, Open, Close, Info, Print, Help and Options.

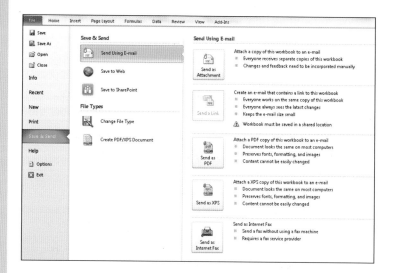

In this figure, Excel is open and Save & Send is selected. This option is available in Word and PowerPoint too. The items that appear on the right change each time you select an option on the left. Note all of the different ways you can send an Excel spreadsheet.

Some options under the File tab open windows. For instance, clicking File and then Save As opens the Save As dialogue box shown here.

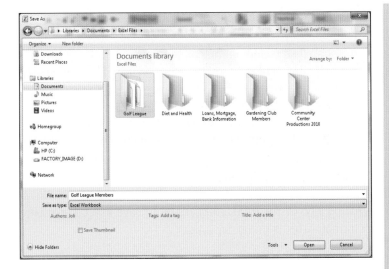

All of the Office programs you'll be working with also offer *Options* under the File tab. From the Options window you can personalise the application. Although there are literally hundreds of ways to make changes, here are a few you'll probably be interested in:

- Show or hide the Mini Toolbar – the Mini Toolbar is the small formatting bar that appears when you select text. If you find this distracts you and you'd rather use the larger and easier-to-see-and-access Font group from the Home tab, you can hide this. (This is under General.)

- Make changes to the colour scheme – the default colour scheme is grey, but if you have enough grey in your life already, opt for blue or black. (This is under General.)

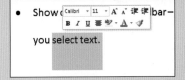

Understand the File tab (cont.)

■ Change AutoCorrect options – Office programs will automatically correct words in its dictionary that you misspell (like changing mispell to misspell), but you can turn off spell check if you like. Alternatively, you can expand or tweak the dictionary by adding your own words. (This is under Proofing.)

■ Save files in a different format – by default, Office programs save files in the newest format available, and these files are only compatible with Office 2007 and Office 2010. If you know you're going to share files with someone who is still using say, Office 2000, you can opt to save in a compatible format. (This is under Save.)

■ Provide feedback with sound – if you have problems with your vision you can tell Office to provide any feedback it has with sound. (This is under Advanced.)

■ Add items to the Quick Access toolbar – the Quick Access toolbar is the small bar located either above or below the Ribbon. It generally has Save, Undo Typing and Redo Typing on it by default. You can add or remove items from Options. (This is under Quick Access Toolbar.) If you have problems seeing what's on the screen, you may not want to use this toolbar, but if your vision is fine, it can be a real help by offering quick access to the commands you use most.

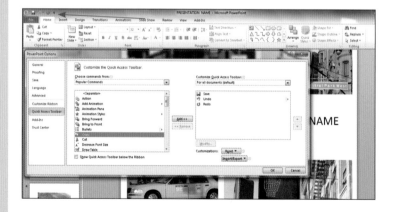

Important

If you make changes to the options here, your version of Office may not look or work exactly like what we describe in the book (such as instructions on using the Mini Toolbar, which won't appear if disabled). For best results, simply browse the options now.

Jargon buster

Control Panel – Available from your computer's Start menu, the Control Panel offers a place to make system-wide changes such as changing the screen resolution, making text larger or smaller, and even adding a second display (to share what's on your screen between two monitors), among other things.

Explore Office Options

1 In Word, Excel or PowerPoint, click the File tab.

2 Click Options.

3 Click each tab on the left side and browse the options that appear on the right.

Add an icon to the Quick Access toolbar

1 Locate the down arrow on Quick Access toolbar.

2 Click any command to add it.

3 To add commands that aren't shown, click More Commands. (Note: You can change where the Quick Access toolbar appears – above or below the Ribbon.)

4 Click any command on the left and click Add to add it to the Quick Access toolbar.

5 Repeat as desired, noting that you can change from where you choose the commands.

6 Click OK.

Explore common features

Introduction

Microsoft Office programs have similarities and commonalities. Once you learn how to perform a task in one program you can perform it in any. You can create new files, add and format text, insert pictures and clip art, and more, and it's all performed in practically the same manner no matter what program you're using.

Everything you create and save in Microsoft Office is a file. Presumably, everything you create also contains text. Thus, files and text are the most logical place to start when learning about Microsoft Office, and the two most important things to understand before you tackle the intricacies of any Office program. Your computer also plays an important role regarding files, and it's imperative to understand where files are saved by default on your PC. You'll learn about this in Chapter 3. Understanding a little about files and where they are saved will help you stay organised, enable you to keep files in a folder where they can easily be backed up, manage them in subfolders, and more. It's very similar to the old filing cabinets you remember – everything has a place.

Once you know a little about files and how to input and format text, you can then begin to perform some of the common tasks that can be achieved in all Office programs. Some tasks are the same no matter what program you're using. For instance, you can add text to any Word document, any

Excel spreadsheet, any PowerPoint slide and any new email by placing the cursor in the appropriate place and typing. You format that text the same way in every program: you select the text and then use the Mini Toolbar, the Home tab (or Message tab in Outlook), or the Font dialogue box. Similarly, once you've found the proper command for inserting a picture, the process of locating the picture to insert is the same no matter what program you're in. In this chapter you'll learn about these things and more, and you'll be well on your way to understanding how the applications in the suite are similar, and how you can apply your learning to all programs in it.

Microsoft Word, Excel and PowerPoint enable you to create new files easily. Files are the things you create, save, email and print. Files contain your data and are stored on your computer's hard drive. When creating a new file, you can create one that's blank or you can select one that already contains some data by selecting an available template. New files are generally created from the File tab of the Ribbon.

Once you have a new file open (or a file you've already opened, saved, closed and reopened), you can then begin to add your own text and numerical data, apply text and data formatting, and add pictures, tables, charts and the like to enhance it.

You can open a file you've previously worked on and saved by clicking Recent instead of New from the File tab. There you'll have access to your most recent files and can double-click them instead of a new file. Here you can see some of my recent files. You may not have any recent files if you're totally new to Microsoft Office.

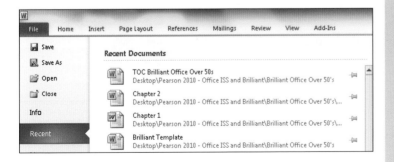

Create a new file

Create a new file in Word

1 Open Microsoft Word.

2 Note that a new, blank document opens.

3 To create a different document type:

a Click the File tab.

b Click New.

c Double-click any file type to open it.

Did you know?

You must be online (connected to the Internet) to open an Office.com template.

Create a new file (cont.)

Create a new presentation in PowerPoint

1 Open Microsoft PowerPoint.

2 Note that a new, blank presentation opens.

3 To create a different presentation type:

   a Click the File tab.

   b Click New.

   c Double-click any file type to open it.

You can open files from your personal folder too. To locate your personal folder, click Start and click your name at the top of the Start menu. Once there you can explore the various folders that likely contain files you've already created. Try the Documents or My Documents folder first. You may see something similar to what's shown here. Simply double-click any file to open it; it will open in the proper program. (Documents will open in Word, spreadsheets in Excel, and presentations in PowerPoint.)

In the figure above, notice that there are subfolders that also contain data. We created these folders; they don't come with the operating system.

With any new file open, it's easy to input data. You can type text, input numbers into tables, or add text to 'text boxes', to name a few. Once you've input this data you can format it in multiple ways to enhance it. Formatting text can include making text bold, adding colour, or changing the size, while formatting data such as numbers, dates and currency can include changing how the numbers are represented on the page. Each program offers similar ways to format data, including using the Mini Toolbar for formatting text, shown here, as well as the Font group available from the Home tab of Word, Excel and PowerPoint.

Type and format text

Use the Mini Toolbar

1 Select any text in any program.

2 Move and position the mouse above the text until you see the Mini Toolbar.

3 Select any item on the toolbar to apply it.

2

Important

If you have trouble with the mouse due to arthritis or some other condition, the Mini Toolbar may not be your cup of tea. You can hide the Mini Toolbar from the File menu by clicking Options. Look in the General tab.

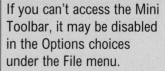

For your information

If you can't access the Mini Toolbar, it may be disabled in the Options choices under the File menu.

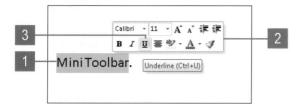

Important

If the Mini Toolbar is enabled and you can view it once but not again, type a few more letters, then deselect and reselect the text. It can be a little finicky.

The most common formatting that you'll likely apply includes:

- Bold – to make text **stand out**.

- Italic – to make text appear *slanted*.

- Underline – to denote the importance of text by <u>underlining</u> it.

Type and format text (cont.)

Use the Font group

1. Open Word, PowerPoint or Excel.
2. Click the Home tab.
3. Select any text to format.
4. In the Font group, click any formatting option to apply it.

- Highlight – to call out specific text as important by highlighting it.
- Font type – to change the look of the text by changing the font type. This is **Berlin Sans FB**, and this is **Broadway**.
- Font size – to increase or decrease the size of the text.
- Font color – to change the font's colour.
- Strikethrough – to show you've ~~deleted text~~ and the reader should note its deletion.

> **Important** !
>
> The Mini Toolbar is just that, it's a mini toolbar. As such it does not contain all of the formatting options available. However, the Font Group does allow access to all of the popular formatting tools listed here.

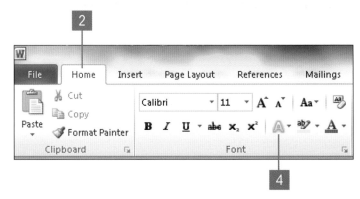

Each program also offers additional formatting options from their own specific tabs. For instance, Microsoft Word has lots of preconfigured 'styles' that you can access from the Home tab. These styles can be used to apply a lot of formatting with a single click. For instance, you can apply the Title Style to quickly create a header for a paper or publication. The formatting includes a font type, font size, font colour, and underlining. If you had to apply all of that it would certainly take more time than clicking it once from the Styles group on Word's Home tab!

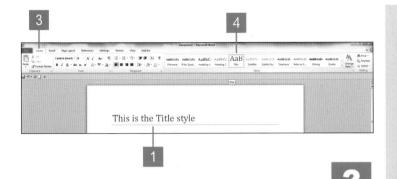

This is the Title style

Did you know?

You can apply a style to only text you've selected, instead of applying it to an entire line or paragraph.

Microsoft PowerPoint has a lot of preconfigured 'themes' that you can access from the Design tab. As with Word's Styles, you can apply an incredible amount of formatting with a single click. Consider the two images here. One is a blank slide; the other is a slide with the 'Austin' theme applied. It would take quite some time to apply all of this formatting yourself.

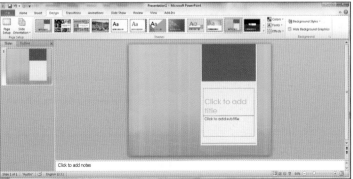

Type and format text (cont.)

Select a Style in Word

1 In Word, type any text.

2 Place your cursor anywhere on the line of text to format.

3 Click the Home tab.

4 Hover over any style in the Styles tab group.

5 When you see a style you like, click it.

Did you know?

You select a theme from the Design tab in PowerPoint the same way you select a style from the Home tab in Word.

Explore common features 23

Type and format text (cont.)

Microsoft Excel has some formatting available too. In Excel, you can apply a theme from the Page Layout tab. You can also apply specific colours, fonts or effects to tweak any theme you've applied. You may use themes less here than in PowerPoint, but they're available if you need them.

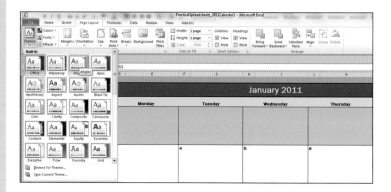

You can apply formatting to data in Excel; this type of formatting you apply to numbers, dates and currency. To access the data formatting options, select any numerical data, right-click it and select Format Cells. From there you can access the type of data you want to change from the left side of the Format Cells dialogue box and select the ideal formatting options on the right.

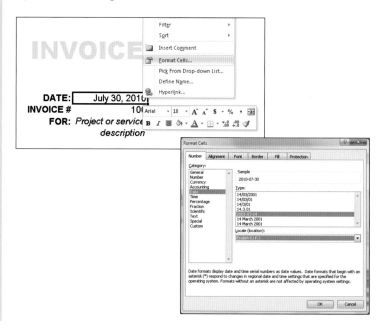

Did you know?

Office programs automatically check your spelling and grammar while you work, but you can run the Spelling and Grammar checker at any time. You'll find these tools under the Review tab.

Apply formatting to numbers

1 In Excel, type 5.32 in any cell.

2 Right-click the cell and Format Cells.

3 Click the Currency tab in the left pane.

4 Select the desired currency format in the right pane.

5 Click OK.

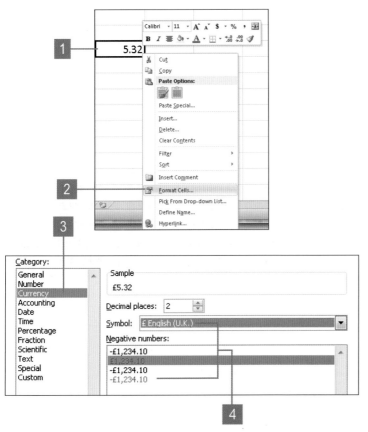

The most common numerical formatting tools include:

■ Number of decimal places

■ Currency symbol

■ Date format

■ Time format.

Work with pictures and clip art

After text and numerical data, pictures and clip art are high on the document/presentation popularity list. Pictures add meaning to files and spice to presentations. Of course, inserting pictures in emails is quite prevalent too, as is adding images and clip art to Excel invoices, time sheets and budgets. No matter what you want to add a picture to, though, it's all done in pretty much the same way. For the most part, you click the Insert tab, select Picture or Clip Art, locate the item to insert, then insert it.

Insert a picture in a PowerPoint slide

1. Open PowerPoint.

2. Click in the slide where you'd like to insert the picture.

3. Click the Insert tab.

4. Click Picture.

5. Locate and double-click the picture to add.

6. Grab the picture by the corner to resize it.

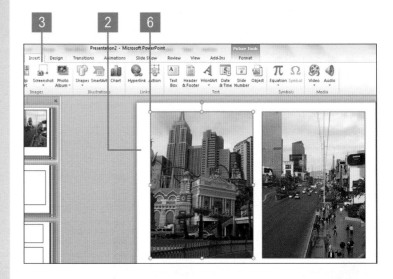

Did you know?

The green circle above the picture is a handle for rotating the picture.

For your information

If you use a slide or template that includes a space for a picture, it will likely be automatically sized to fit, as shown in this figure.

After you've inserted a picture, you'll have access to the Picture Tools tab. This tab only appears after you've inserted a picture and selected it. (When you click off the picture, or deselect it, the Picture Tools tab disappears.) You can make lots of edits to a picture using these tools, including but not limited to:

- Correcting the picture colour – you can change the saturation, colour tone, temperature, and even recolour the image.

- Adjusting the sharpness – you can sharpen and soften a picture, or change the brightness or contrast.

- Applying artistic effects – you can completely change the picture by making it look like a chalk drawing, oil painting and other artwork. 'Glow Edges' is shown here.

2

Did you know?

After inserting a picture (and clicking on it) a new tab will appear: Picture Tools.

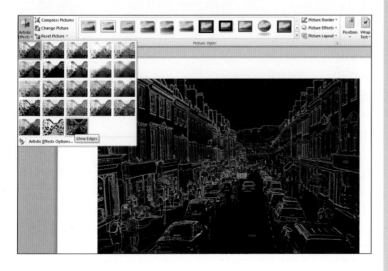

Work with pictures and clip art (cont.)

Edit a picture in Word

1 Open Word and insert a picture using the techniques detailed for PowerPoint.

2 Click the picture once.

3 Click the Picture Tools tab.

4 Click the down arrows on the tab to explore the options.

5 Click various options from the Styles group.

■ Adding a frame – from the Styles group you can apply a picture border and set the characteristics for it.

■ Crop – you can crop out parts of the picture you do not want.

Important

It's best to edit your pictures before inserting them in any Office program using a graphics-editing program such as Windows Live Photo Gallery, Photoshop or Photoshop Elements, because in comparison, Microsoft Office programs don't offer much in the way of editing.

For your information

You have access to photo-editing tools after you insert a picture in an email in Outlook too.

Important

The more time you spend exploring the options the better! Not only will you familiarise yourself with the Picture Tools options, but you'll also learn how to use the down arrows, menus and other options work.

You may not think you'd do much picture editing in Excel, and you're probably right. Although you might insert a picture to serve as a company logo in the top right or left corner of the page, you'll likely do much more with pictures in Word, PowerPoint and Outlook. However, you may find that inserting and editing clip art is quite useful in Excel, under specific circumstances. You can add clip art to invoices, inventory sheets, calendars, labels, memos and all kinds of other Excel worksheets. Although it doesn't often serve any 'purpose', it can enhance the look and feel of a worksheet.

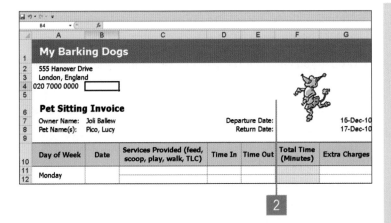

2

The clip art we'll use here comes from Office.com. This means you'll have to be connected to the Internet to access it. When searching through Office.com you can opt to search all media files, or a combination of illustrations, photographs, videos and audio.

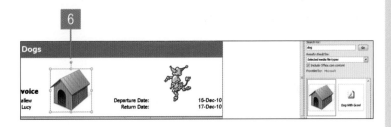

6

Insert clip art in Excel

1 Open Excel.

2 Click near where you'd like to insert the clip art.

3 Click the Insert tab and click Clip Art.

4 Browse through the available clip art.

5 Double-click the clip art to add.

6 Position the clip art by dragging it and resize it using the 'handles' on the corners.

For your information

As you can see here, when searching for clip art you may also see media files and other types of data.
If you only want to search clip art, under Results, click Illustrations.

Work with tables

Tables are one of the greatest features of Microsoft Office. You can use tables to easily organise data, to make lists of data easier to read and manage, and even just to break up a page of text. But there's much more to it than that. Once you've created a table you can remove the 'borders', so no one can tell it ever *was* a table! The result looks like you spent hours creating the perfect tab stops to align your data, when in reality you simply input the data in a table you created in Microsoft Office and hid the table borders. Once you've created a table (provided you want to show the table and not just use it for formatting text), you can change the style, border, layout, colour, thickness of the lines and more.

Insert a table

1 Open Word.

2 Click the Insert tab.

3 Click the arrow under Table.

4 Drag your mouse to select the table size.

5 Click once.

Important

It's best to learn how to work with tables in Word, Outlook or PowerPoint first, because tables in Excel are a bit more complicated, include formulas and often have very specific uses.

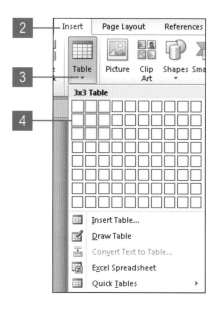

After you've input a table and clicked in it, the Table Tools tab appears, and with it two subtabs: Design and Layout. You can use these tabs to personalise the look of the table. Although there are several ways you can format your table using these, here are the most common uses:

■ Select a table style – from the Design tab, you can select a style that contains formatting including colour, line and separator type, and row and column structuring.

■ Change the table style options – from the Design tab, you can remove or add various options to the style you've selected, including 'banding' – adding colour to various rows and columns.

■ Shading and Borders – from the Design tab, you can use these features to change the shade or add borders to an entire table, a single cell or multiple cells. You should select the desired area of the table before applying the formatting.

■ View or hide gridlines – from the Layout tab, you can show or hide the lines in the table.

■ Insert or delete rows or columns – from the Layout tab you can edit the table by adding or removing rows and columns.

■ Align – from the Layout tab you can state how data should be aligned in a cell in a table. You'll find the usual alignment options, including left, centre and right, along with top, centre and bottom.

Jargon buster

Cell: a single 'box' in a table.

Input data into a cell or table

1 Click inside any cell.

2 Type in the desired data.

3 Use the tab key to move from cell to cell.

4 Use the mouse to click any cell.

5 Click and drag to select cells you want to format.

Work with tables (cont.)

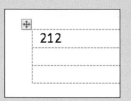

Did you know?

You can also select the entire table from the Design Tool's Layout tab under Select.

Once you've started work on a table, you may find that you need to insert rows or columns, or delete them. You'll also want to remove borders or enhance them. All of these things are achieved from the Table Tools tabs. It'll be best for you to explore these on your own and as we progress through the book, but here are a few pointers to help get you started:

■ To select an entire table – position the mouse in the top left corner until you see the four-headed arrow. Click it. You'll need to select the entire table to apply formatting to the entire table.

■ To hide the table and only show the data in it – select the entire table, and from the Design tab, under Borders, click No Border.

■ To quickly format a table with colour, borders, fonts and more – select the entire table and from the Design tab, select a Table Style.

■ To insert rows – click inside the row below where you want the new row to be added. From the Layout tab, click Insert Above. (Note: you can also choose Insert Below.)

■ To insert columns – click to the left of where you want the new column to be added. From the Layout tab, click Insert Left. (Note: you can also choose Insert Right.)

Important

If you decide to delete the table after inserting it, you can't just select it and click Delete on the keyboard; that only deletes the table data. Instead, right-click the four-headed arrow that appears when you position your mouse in the top left corner of the table and from the resulting options, click Delete Table.

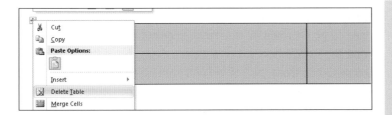

You can draw your own table or insert a 'Quick Table', if you need to configure a table quickly. A Quick Table is a kind of table template complete with formatting, text and data already included, and you can easily personalise it to suit your needs. Once you've inserted a Quick Table, you can replace the data that is already included with your own. Be creative! Just because a table contains data about the number of students at a university in a given year, as shown here, doesn't mean it can't be edited to show how many people you had in the community centre group last year, this year and the change.

Insert a quick table

1 Open Word.

2 Click the Insert tab.

3 Click the arrow under Table.

4 Click Quick Tables.

5 Choose and click a table to insert.

2

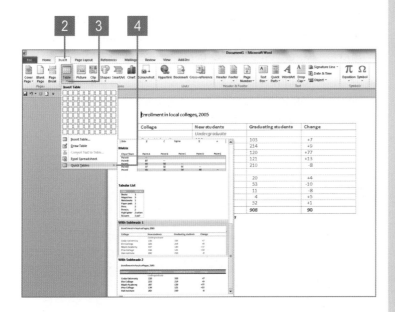

Save, Share and Print

Introduction

It's important that you understand where files are saved by
default, how and why you should continue to save them there,
and how to keep your files organised in the long term. This
involves understanding how to create your own subfolders and
moving files into them, as well as how to rename and delete
files you've previously saved. You'll also want to share files,
perhaps by emailing, perhaps by printing or perhaps by saving
them to a repository on the internet. No matter what program
you're using, these ideas and tasks are universal. Once you're
finished here, you'll be ready to move on to the chapters that
introduce the program you'd like to learn more about and you
can skip around the rest of the book as desired.

What you'll do

Work with files

Organise files

Share and print files

Email a file

Print files

Work with files

When you create something in Word, Excel or PowerPoint, you save it. What you save is called a file. You can open a saved file to view or edit it later, and you can share the file by printing it, emailing it, faxing it and more. Files are stored on the hard drive of your computer, in folders and subfolders.

You already have some knowledge to draw from regarding files, computers and hard drives if you've ever used a filing cabinet. With a filing cabinet, you print and then file the documents, presentations and spreadsheets you create. You file those documents in folders and subfolders that you also create and name. You decide on the type of filing system, how to organise your files and you know exactly how to pull them from a folder when you need them. You do the same with files on your computer. You can create folders called Travel, Taxes, Health, Kids, etc., and file data into them to organise it.

In this section you'll learn a little about your computer, including where files are saved by default, how to save a file and where and how to organise the files you want to keep. In order to avoid being overwhelmed later by data you've amassed, you must also understand how to delete or rename files as well. We won't spend an inordinate amount of time on this here; instead, you'll learn just enough to get you started. To learn more, consider a book like *Computer Basics Windows 7 Edition*, also published by Prentice-Hall.

Save a file

On Microsoft computers you're prompted to save files in the default folders that are already created for you. These include My Documents, My Pictures, My Videos and so on, as well as their 'public' counterparts. Similar folders exist on Macs. You should save your files to these folders for lots of reasons. First, you'll know where to find them. If your documents are in the My Documents folder, well, it's easy to locate them. Second, when you use any backup program, it'll automatically back up what's in these folders so you won't have to be concerned whether or not your data is being backed up. And finally, you can personalise these folders with subfolders that work for you, like Golf Club, Football Pool, Presentations, Budgets and the like. The first step in utilising these folders is to save a file there.

1c

For your information

The first time you click Save or Save As, the Save As dialogue box opens. There, you can choose where and how to save your file. To save changes you've made to an already saved file, simply click the Save icon on the Quick Access toolbar or Save from the File menu. (Clicking Save As a second time opens the Save As dialogue box again, which is unnecessary.)

Once you've saved a file, you have to browse to it the next time you want to access it. There are several ways to do this, but one is to click the Start menu and click your user name. This folder contains all of your personal data. Alternatively, you can click Start and then click Documents, Pictures or even Recent Items.

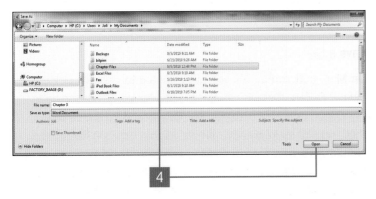

4

Finally, with Windows Vista and Windows 7, you can also type part of the file name in the Start Search window to locate a file, and the results will appear in the Start menu. No matter how you locate the file, you simply double-click the file to open it. It will open in the program associated with it.

Save a File

1 In any Office program, perform any of the following steps:

   a Click the Save icon on the Quick Launch toolbar.

   b Click the File tab, and click Save.

   c Click the File tab, and click Save As.

2 In the Save As dialogue box, type a name for the file.

3 Use the down arrow to select the file type (although the default is almost always fine).

4 Locate the folder on the hard drive where you'd like to save the file and click Open. Look for the Documents library or the My Documents folder.

5 Click Save.

3

Important

If you can't locate the proper folder, click Documents in the left pane.

Work with files (cont.)

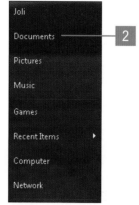

Open and edit a file

1. Click Start.

2. Click Documents.

3. Double-click the file to open it.

4. If you don't see the file:

   a Double-click the subfolder you saved it to.

   Or close this window and then:

   b Click Start, and in the Start Search window, type part of the file name.

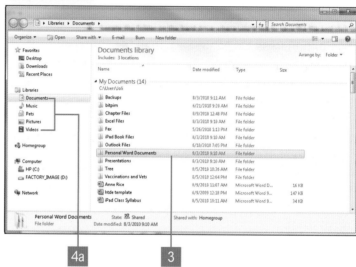

> ### ! Important
>
> The steps here and throughout the rest of this section are written with Windows 7 in mind, but you can perform the same steps with other operating systems.

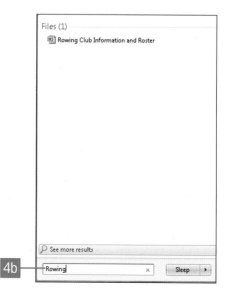

Organising your folders, subfolders and files is pretty easy. You can create the appropriate subfolders with only a few clicks of the mouse. It's equally easy to name a file with something descriptive and save it to the proper folder each time you create something new. It takes discipline to do this all of the time, though, and to continually create subfolders to stay organised, and it takes nerve to be able to delete files you no longer need.

To organise the files you want to keep and to make it easier to stay organised for the long term, consider your interests and what you create files for. If you give a lot of presentations as a consultant or educator, create folders for each presentation or lesson that you create. In that subfolder you can keep the PowerPoint presentations, the Excel file that contains the attendee information and pictures you use in your presentations and lessons. If you travel quite a bit, consider a Travel subfolder and subfolders in it for each destination. If you play a lot of sports, consider a Sports folder and subfolders in it for each sport you play. Likewise, if you have a lot of grandchildren, create a subfolder for each.

Important

Notice in the figure here that there's a subfolder named Excel Files in the Documents library. In that subfolder are five more, along with a stray Excel file.

After you create the desired subfolders, you should move any files that are currently misplaced into them. There are many ways to move files, but the easiest is to 'cut' the file from its current folder and then 'paste' it to the desired one. You can access these commands by right-clicking the file.

You can also move multiple files at one time. To select contiguous files, hold the Shift key down while selecting the first and last file in a list. This will select all the files in between. To select non-contiguous files, hold down the Ctrl key while selecting. Then, click each file separately to add it

Organise files

Create subfolders

1 Open the Documents folder.

2 Click New Folder.

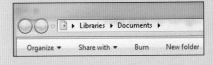

3 Name the folder.

4 Click Enter on the keyboard.

For your information

If something happens during the naming process and the new subfolder takes on the name New Folder, right-click it and click Rename. Then try again.

Organise files (cont.)

Move files with Cut and Paste

1 Locate the files to move and select them.

2 Right-click the files and click Cut.

3 Locate the folder to which you'd like to move the files.

4 Right-click inside that folder and click Paste.

to the set. With the files selected, you can then right-click and choose Cut, locate the appropriate subfolder and right-click and choose Paste.

Beyond cutting and pasting, you can position windows side by side on your computer screen, one window for one folder and the other window for another, and drag files to move them. This requires you open both windows and position them, which can be done using the new Windows 7 'snap' feature, but can prove difficult if you aren't very knowledgeable about how the folders on your computer are organised. It's an option, though.

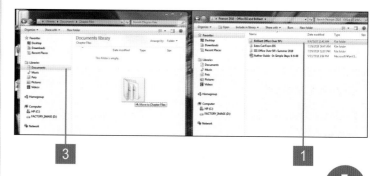

For your information

There's the option to Copy instead of Cut when right-clicking data. When you choose Copy, you create a copy of the data that can then be pasted. Creating copies of data on the same computer causes headaches though, because you have duplicate files on a single PC and you'll have a hard time keeping track of what edits have been applied to which file, and which file contains the most recent information. It's best to move data and not copy it. Save copying data for backing it up.

Finally, you'll want to keep files organised by renaming them if their file name does not describe what's in the file, or if you've edited the file such that the current name no longer suits it. You'll also need to delete files you no longer need. Consider deleting files that contain:

- To-do lists that have been completed.

- Quick notes to yourself.

- Grocery or shopping lists.

- Driving directions you printed and used once (and won't need again).

- Anything else you are sure you'll never need again.

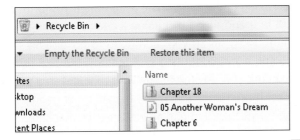

Did you know?

Deleted files are stored in the Recycle Bin until you empty it.

Organise files (cont.)

Rename and delete files

1 Right-click any file name to rename or delete it.

2 To rename a file, click Rename and then type the new name of the file.

3 To delete a file, click Delete and click Yes to verify this.

3

Did you know?

Files you delete remain in the Windows Recycle Bin until you empty it. If you ever accidentally delete a file, open the Recycle Bin, locate the file and click Restore.

Share and print files

Although you will often create documents, notes, lists and spreadsheets for your eyes only, there will be times when you want to share the files you create. You can share a PowerPoint presentation by projecting it onto a big screen and you can share slideshows you create by showing them on a computer. (If you have a Windows 7 HomeGroup and compliant devices, you can even play them 'to' those devices from your computer!) But for the most part, sharing involves emailing and printing, although it can also include faxing, uploading to a website, or sending to a shared office portal.

Printing and emailing are the same for Word, Excel and PowerPoint. As you'd expect, printing in Outlook is the same, but because the program's main purpose is to allow you to correspond using email, that particular function is a bit different. Faxing is the same in all programs if you print the document first and then fax it using a dedicated fax machine. However, you can set up your computer to fax directly from Windows and skip the printing step entirely, but this requires you to connect your PC (complete with modem) to a phone line and set it up. Hence this is the reason most people print out a document then and use a dedicated fax machine.

Regarding the other options you'll see when you click the File tab, you'll see options Save to Web, Save to SharePoint, and depending on the program you're using, other options. In PowerPoint, shown here, you can package the presentation for burning to a CD, create a video, create handouts and more. You're welcome to explore these additional options on your own, including saving to the web. Don't worry, you'll be prompted regarding any steps required to complete the task.

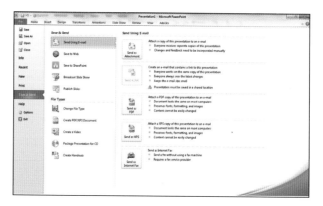

You can choose to email a file from Word, Excel or PowerPoint, you can tell the program to package the file as an attachment and attach it to a new email using Outlook. (You can also have it perform other actions, such as changing the file to a PDF before attaching it, so the recipient won't be able to edit it easily.) If you have not yet set up Outlook, you'll be prompted to do so at this time. So, if you have not set up an email program, you may want to skip this part of the chapter until you do.

When you opt to email a file, you have several options:

- Send as attachment – this is the format you're likely familiar with. The file is attached to the email and has a paper clip icon, and each recipient gets their own copy. If you're going to have those people edit the document, you'll have to incorporate all of those edits manually. If you simply want to share a file and you don't care what your readers do with it, this is the way to go, though.

- Send a link – this option will be greyed out unless you've saved the file to a shared location, such as a company web server. If you choose this option, everyone works on the same copy, if edits are indeed required. This is a good option if a shared location is available and if editing is necessary.

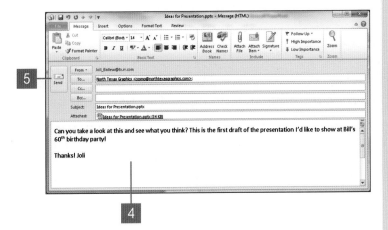

Email a file

Send a file as an email attachment

1 In Word, Excel or PowerPoint, click the File tab.

2 Click Save & Send and Send Using E-Mail.

3 Click Send as Attachment (or another choice as applicable).

4 Complete the email as desired.

5 Click Send.

3

Did you know?

The Subject line in the email will contain the name of the file. You may want to change this to better represent what the email is about.

Email a file (cont.)

- Send as PDF – this is a great option for sending invoices, flyers, brochures and other items that are in their final form. It's difficult to edit a PDF file that's been sent in an email. Also, fonts that are used in the file are 'embedded', unlike fonts used in, say, a Word document sent as an attachment. Additionally, formatting and images are preserved. This means that what you create and send is what the recipient sees. (In a Word document sent as an attachment, fonts are substituted at the recipient's end if the font is not already installed on their computer, and formatting and images can be lost as well.) You can think of a PDF as a kind of snapshot of your document or file.

- Send as XPS – similar to a PDF file, this option preserves fonts, formatting and images, and cannot be easily edited.

- Send as Internet Fax – although not technically an email, if you've set up your computer to act as a fax machine, opt for this when you need to fax the file. Otherwise you'll have to print the document and fax it using a fax machine.

While the command to print is the same for all of the Office programs, printing is a delicate process, especially if you're dealing with multi-page Excel worksheets or long PowerPoint presentations that also contain handouts. If you're simply printing a Word document, it's easy. You simply select a printer, choose the number of copies, and generally that's it. Nothing to it! If you only want to print a single page of a larger file, though, a colour photograph, brochure or flyer, or if you need to print handouts, collate the copies or print on both sides of the paper, you've got a little more work to do.

You'll find the options you need under the File menu in any Office program. The options you see will depend on what program you're using. Here's Outlook, followed by Word.

3

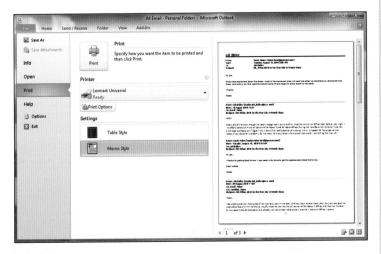

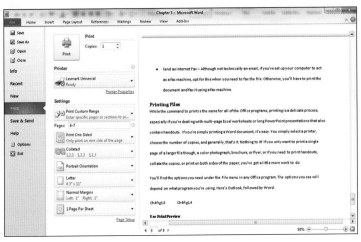

Print files (cont.)

And for the sake of completeness, here's PowerPoint and Excel, although these two shots only show the options and do not show the preview pane. As you can see, each program offers a File tab, and each a Print option. In the Print option, you can preview the print.

Use Print Preview

1 Open the file to print.

2 Click the File tab.

3 Click Print in the left pane.

4 Notice the preview pane to the right.

5 Verify first that the image fits inside the printing area.

6 Next, you can configure settings.

Choose Print Settings

1 Open the file to print.

2 Click the File tab.

3 Click Print.

4 Select the printer to use from the Printer options.

5 Under Settings, click the arrows for each as applicable, and review the options.

6 Select options as applicable.

7 To print only specific pages or slides, type the data to print using something similar to this: 1–3, 4, 6–10.

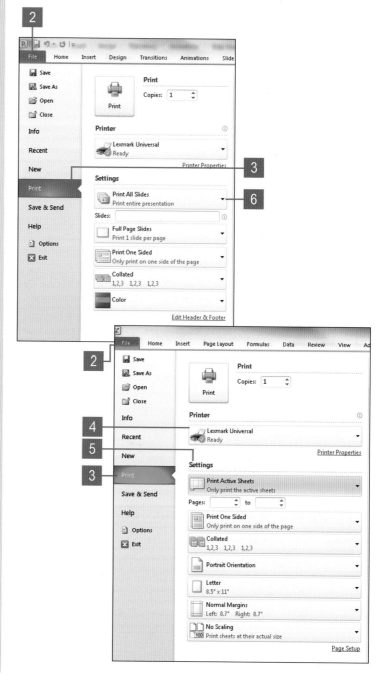

You probably noticed in these images that there are myriad Print options. We won't discuss all of the options here, though; that will be up to you to explore and the options can be dependent on the printer you own. (Not all printers can print on both sides of the paper, for instance, and some printers don't print in colour.)

Here are some common print options to explore, organised by the task you'd want to perform (not the command name you'll see in the interface):

- Choose a printer – if you have multiple printers attached to your PC or available from your network, you can choose the one you want to use.
- Choose a print range – you can print all worksheets in Excel or only active ones, all slides in a PowerPoint presentation or only specific ones, all pages in an email in Outlook or only specific ones, or all pages in a document or only ones you select.
- Collated or not collated – when printing multiple copies of a multi-page document, presentation or worksheet, you have the option to collate the copies. Collating means the printer will print all pages of a file at once, and then start again to print the next copy, and the next. If you do not collate copies, the printer will print the desired number of pages for page 1, repeat for page 2, etc.
- Colour, grey scale or black and white – if your printer supports it, you can print a file in colour, using grey scale, or using black and white only.

Important !

Before you print the file, note how many pages the file contains. This is shown in the preview window on the right side, towards the bottom. If you only need to print the first page, last page, or a group of pages, understand that you can state which pages to print in the print options.

3

i

For your information

In the Pages or Slides option for stating the pages to print, if you type, say, 1–3, 4, 6–10, you're telling the printer to print pages 1, 2 and 3, page 4 and pages 6–10. The same holds true when you select specific slides.

Print files (cont.)

Print a file

1. Open the file to print and access the Print command.

2. Verify the proper printer is selected.

3. Verify the printer is 'online'.

4. Verify the settings.

5. Verify the pages to print.

6. Click OK and then click Print.

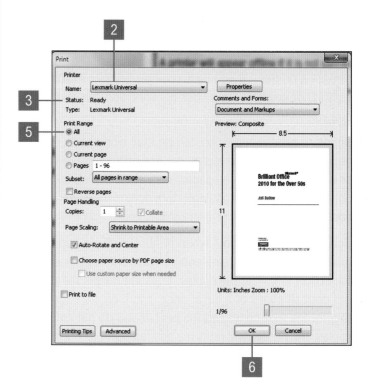

Word basics

Introduction

Microsoft Word is a program you use to create Word documents. Documents can be created for just about anything, including simple letters or faxes, signs for lost pets or items for sale, family newsletters (complete with pictures), multi-page brochures for a new product or business or a playbill for a production you're a part of at the local drama group. Because you can easily copy and paste, you can also create your own itineraries for travel, complete with pictures you copy from websites. There's no end to what you can produce.

You've already learned how to do quite a few things in Word that are universal to all programs, including changing font characteristics, saving and reopening a file, adding items to the Quick Access toolbar, typing text, using the Mini Toolbar and even inserting things like clip art, pictures and tables. You can use that knowledge as a starting point for this chapter. Additionally, Microsoft Word, like the other applications in the Microsoft Office suite, has tabs across the top of the page and a Ribbon that changes each time you select one of those tabs. There are tabs that enable you to save, open and print documents (File), format text and align paragraphs (Home), insert pictures, clip art, shapes and the like (Insert), and more.

What you'll do

Work in a document

Explore views

Use Zoom

Move around in a document

Edit text

Select text

Undo Use Typing and Redo Typing

Use Find and Replace

Create bulleted and numbered lists

Use the Format Painter

Explore templates

Important

If you didn't read Chapters 1, 2 and 3, you should do that now. Those chapters introduced tasks that can be applied to almost every program in the Microsoft Office Suite, and are necessary knowledge to get the most from this book.

Work in a document

You have already learned a little about the Word interface. You know it has a Ribbon, and that Ribbon has tabs you can click. When you click a tab, the items on the Ribbon change to reflect the features available under it. You've used the File tab to save a file, and the Insert tab to insert clip art, and you can likely glean how you'd use other tabs to perform other tasks.

Jargon buster

Document – Word files are called documents, for the most part. Depending on what you create, you may call the file a brochure, flyer or something equally representative. Here, though, we'll use the word 'document' to represent what we create in Word.

What you haven't really explored is the part of Word where you type; the larger area under the Ribbon. This is the body. This area will have scroll bars when the document is longer than can be viewed on the screen, has the option to zoom using a slider located at the bottom of the page and offers various views for reading and working in Word. You can also show various features, including a ruler.

Word offers several ways to view documents on your computer screen. There's Print Layout, Full Screen Reading, Web Layout, Outline and Draft, and you can opt to show or hide the Ruler, gridlines or the Navigation pane. You may find you like one view over another for specific tasks. You access these options from Word's View tab.

You can also switch between views from the Status bar. The Status bar is the small thin bar that runs across the bottom of the Word interface and is shown here. Print Layout is selected. The only problem we can see with using the Status bar to switch views is just that, you can't see it! The icons are extremely small. However, if your eyesight is still 20–20, you may find that using this option is better than using the View menu, because you never have to switch tabs to access it.

We're focusing on Print Layout view mostly because with Print Layout, what you see on the screen is what you'll see when the document is printed. This is a nice option because you know you won't be surprised when you decide to print. What you see is what you get.

There are other views to explore, though. Full Screen reading shows the document as shown here, allowing you to read a document more comfortably. Note that under View Options, also shown, you can increase the text size, show one page instead of two and even allow typing (which is disabled by default). This is ultimately a 'reading' mode, since there's no

For your information

Print Layout seems to be the best view for composing a document flyer or brochure.

Explore views (cont.)

easy access to the Ribbon and other features. To exit this mode, click Close. Word will not close, only the Full Screen reading mode.

Explore different views in the Word window

1. In any document, click the View tab.
2. Click Print Layout.
3. Click Full Screen Reading.
4. Click the Esc key to return to the previous view.
5. Click Web Layout.
6. Click Outline.
7. Click Close Outline View to close it.
8. Click Draft.
9. Click Print Layout to return to the previous view.
10. Click Ruler, Gridlines and Navigation Pane, then deselect these options.

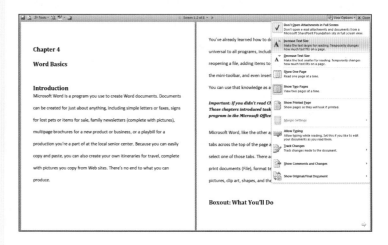

Did you know?

While in Full Screen mode you can click Esc on the keyboard to exit.

Important

Try Outline view if your document has headings and subheadings and you want to review the hierarchy of headings.

There are a few other modes to explore:

▦ Web Layout – enables you to view the document as it would appear on a web page. If you're using Word to create pages for the web, this is a good option.

▦ Outline – enables you to view the document as an outline and offers easy access to the outlining tools, including expanding or collapsing selected items and showing only specific levels of headings in the document. (To exit this view, click Close Outline View.)

▦ Draft – enables you to view the document as a draft to quickly edit text. Some elements, such as headings and footers, will be hidden to make editing easier.

Did you know?

You should show the Ruler when you need to align pictures or clip art.

4

Use Zoom

If you're having trouble seeing what's on the screen, you can use the slider across the bottom to increase the page width. It's a pretty small slider, though, and if you have trouble using the mouse or seeing what's on the Status bar, you may not want to use this feature. If that's the case, you can use Zoom from the View menu. Zoom lets you increase the size by a specific percentage, and offers larger options for doing so. Click the Zoom icon on the View menu to open the dialogue box here, where you can select a specific zoom size or type your own percentage.

Use Zoom

1 From the View tab, click Zoom.

2 Experiment with different Zoom views, clicking OK to apply.

3 Use the slider at the bottom of the interface to change how large the document appears on your screen. Try 100%, 150% and 200%.

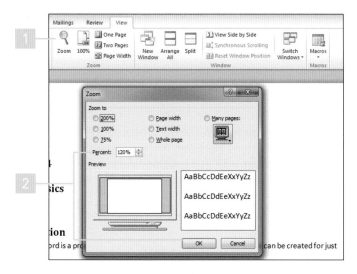

Did you know?

If you have two documents open at the same time, you can view them side by side. Side By Side is an option from the View tab.

Did you know?

From the Zoom dialogue box you can also select Page width, Text width or Whole page. If you have difficulty reading what's on the screen, try Text width first.

Important

If you need to zoom in on a photo or page element, you can set the Zoom to 200 per cent and use the scroll bars to move around in the document.

There are lots of ways to move around in a document, and you're likely aware of the most popular one: simply place the mouse cursor anywhere in the document you desire. Getting there is the fun part. There are several ways to locate a specific place in a document.

- Scroll bars – depending on the length of your document, its size and how much 'zoom' you've applied, you may see one or two toolbars. You can use the toolbars to locate any part of the document quickly.

- Arrow keys – click the arrow keys on the keyboard to move the cursor up or down one line of text, and left and right one character.

- Home and End – if your keyboard has a Home and End key, click them to see what happens. Home may take you to the beginning of a sentence or paragraph, or it may take you to the top of the document. End may have similar features.

- Page Up and Page Down – if your keyboard has these features, use them to move up a page or down one quickly.

- Tab – use the Tab key to move around in a table or move the cursor forward to the next tab stop setting in a document.

Did you know?

You can configure your own tab stops from the Page Layout tab in Word.

Edit text

Most text that you type will need to be edited in one way or another. You may need to apply a style, change the font size, replace a word or change the font colour. You may need to rewrite sentences or entire paragraphs, or you may only need to replace a single word. You may even want to change paragraphs into bulleted or numbered lists. Editing is prevalent because most people opt to get the words down on the paper first, proofread it and make changes to the content second, and then apply formatting third. All of these things are editing tasks and thus require you to understand how to select and edit text in various ways.

Important

When sending a letter to a person who is visually impaired, use a large font. When sending a letter to a person with cognitive difficulties, try a large font combined with very short sentences.

More often than not, you'll opt to select text and improve on it, versus starting over. There are lots of tricks for selecting text, as well as a few tried-and-true favourites.

Select text

■ Drag the cursor – hold down the left mouse button and drag the mouse over the text to select. This is the most commonly used selection option. You can now delete the text, cut or copy the text so you can paste it somewhere else or type over the text.

■ Click twice – click twice on a word to select it. With the word selected you can then type over the word or right-click it to access other options. Synonyms is a great way to find a replacement word, if that's what you're looking for.

■ Click three times – click three times to select the entire sentence or paragraph. You can then right-click the text to apply a style as shown on the next page, as shown in the image below.

■ Click Select from the Home tab – click Select from the Home tab to select the entire document, objects or all text with similar formatting.

See also

Cut, Copy and Paste text later in this chapter.

Timesaver tip

After selecting text you can right-click that text to access the Cut and Copy commands. Cut, Copy and Paste were introduced in Chapter 3 with regard to cutting, copying and pasting entire files and folders, but the same technique and theory apply to text as well.

4

Jargon buster

Cut – to remove text so that you can place it (paste it) somewhere else. (To delete text without the option of pasting later, select it and then click Delete on the keyboard.)

Copy – to copy text so that you can place it (paste it) somewhere else. The original text remains in place.

Paste – to insert text somewhere else that you've previously cut or copied (the same document, a new document, an email, a presentation or just about anywhere).

Select text (cont.)

Select text in various ways

1. Type a sentence.

2. Click twice on a single word to select it.

3. Right-click the word to view your editing options. Notice the options to:

   a Cut and copy

   b Select a new font

   c Apply bullets and numbering

   d Find a synonym.

4. Triple-click the sentence.

5. Right-click again to review your editing options.

Cut, Copy and Paste text

1. Select any text in a document.

2. From the Home tab, click Cut or Copy. Alternatively, right-click the text and choose Cut or Copy.

3. Place the cursor where you'd like to paste the text.

4. From the Home tab, click Paste. Alternatively, right-click and select Paste.

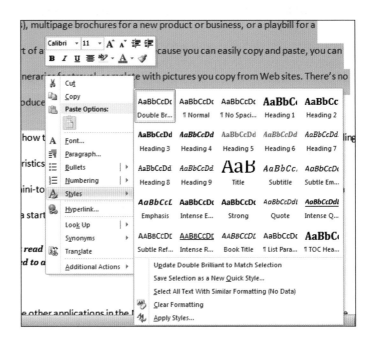

The Quick Access toolbar is the toolbar that contains the icons for Save, Undo Typing and Repeat Typing. (It also contains a down-facing arrow that offers a list of commands you can add to that toolbar quickly.) The Undo Typing command lets you, well, undo the latest words you've typed. You can click Undo repeatedly, because Word keeps track of a long list of past edits. You can use Repeat Typing to undo an 'Undo Typing' command or to retype something you've previously typed.

Did you know?

Undo Typing is not available when you first open a document, even if there's text in it and you've obviously typed something on a previous occasion. Undo Typing is only available on your latest edits to the document during a single writing session.

Did you know?

When you click the Save icon on the Quick Access toolbar, the Redo Typing button becomes greyed out until you type something again.

Use Undo Typing and Redo Typing

Use Undo and Redo Typing commands

1. In any Word document, type some text.

2. Click the Undo Typing button.

3. Click the Undo Typing button again.

4. Click Redo Typing.

5. Click the arrow next to Undo Typing.

6. Use your mouse to select multiple Undo points.

7. Click the last one selected to undo all previous typing to that point. (Click Redo Typing continuously to put it back.)

Use Find and Replace

There will be times when you need to locate and replace a word throughout an entire document. Perhaps one cast member has been substituted for another in a play you're directing, you've decided to change the name of your invention or business, or you're using a template with boilerplate data you'd like to replace. The latter is a very common reason to use Find and Replace; here's an example.

This business card template is from Office.com. Note that the design for the card has already been created, and the spacing is such that the cards can be printed on a specific label sheet that you can buy from an office supply store. Once you've populated the data, you simply print the cards right from your own printer. All you need to do is input your personal information. Instead of inputting all of the data manually (in this instance, 10 times), or even taking a shortcut by inputting the data once and then using Copy and Paste to fill in the rest, you can use the Find and Replace commands to perform the task of populating the cards easily. This option is much faster than any other.

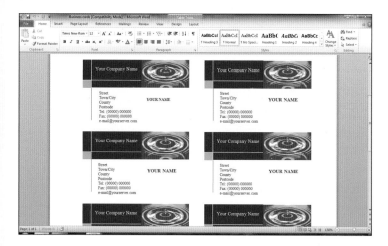

You access the Find and Replace dialogue box by clicking Replace in the top right corner of the Home tab in Word. You'll find this same option and command in other programs too.

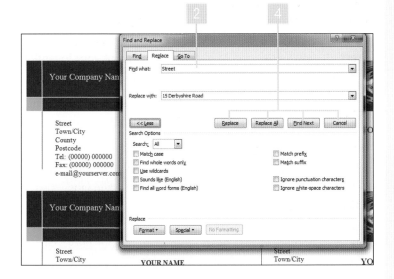

Did you know?

To simply locate a word in a document, click Find instead of Replace in Step 1.

Use Find and Replace

On the Home tab, click Replace.

Type what you'd like to find in Find what:, and type what you'd like to replace it with in Replace with:.

Click More to access more options.

Click any of the following:

a Find Next – to find the next instance of the word(s) and then choose to replace it or not.

b Replace – to replace an instance of a word(s) you've found using Find Next.

c Replace All – to replace all instances of the word(s) in the document.

d Cancel – to close the window and not make any changes.

Click OK in the resulting dialogue box that states how many replacements were made.

Create bulleted and numbered lists

Bulleted and numbered lists can help you organise data in a document. Generally, numbered lists are used to denote the order in which something must be done, while bulleted lists are reserved for features, options, or lists of things that can be done or viewed in any order. You can create these lists from any Microsoft Office program. In Word, Excel and PowerPoint, look for these options on the Home tab. In Outlook, in an email, look to the Message tab. Note that you must have clicked in the body of the email for them to be accessible (since you can't add lists to the Subject line or To: line).

There are several ways to start these lists. For a numbered list, the easiest way is to type the number 1 at the beginning of any line and place a full stop after it. A list will start automatically. To create a bulleted list, type an asterisk (*) and then the Tab key. Both of these techniques will work as long as you have not changed the default settings in the program, because the defaults are to create these lists automatically when you type the 'triggers' for them.

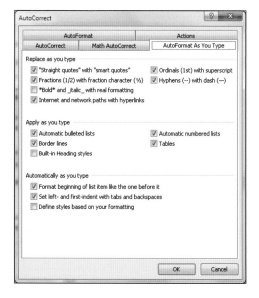

There are other ways. You can also type the list of items first, placing one item on each line, and then select the items with the mouse. Then click the type of list you want to apply to it from the appropriate tab. Additionally, you can select the type of list to create from the Ribbon first, and then type the data second.

The advantage to using the Home tab to create your list (over other options) is that you can select what type of list you want to create instead of simply accepting the defaults. For instance, if you click the arrow next to the Bulleted List icon, you can select the type of bullet to create. The same is true for numbered lists. (Note that None is the default, and is selected when you open the options.)

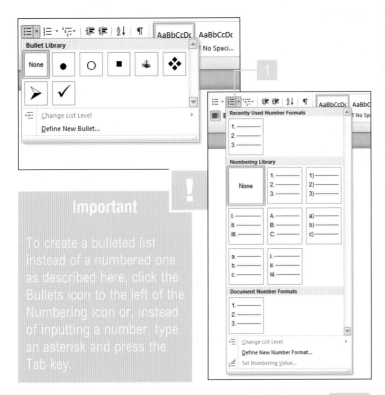

Create bulleted and numbered lists (cont.)

Create a numbered list

1. In Word, from the Home tab, in the Paragraph group, click the Numbering icon.

2. Type your first list item and press Enter or Return on the keyboard.

3. Continue as desired.

4. To stop creating list items, click Enter or the keyboard two times or click the numbering icon on the Home tab.

Did you know?

Depending on your situation, you may see the lightning bolt icon shown here. Click it to see additional options.

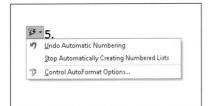

Create bulleted and numbered lists (cont.)

Sometimes you'll want to create more specialised lists. You may want to create a list that has 'heads', such as the number 1 as 'Head 1', followed by an indented a, b and c for 'Head 2', followed by the option to add more of these heads including i, ii and iii. You can do this, again, in various ways. One way is this: instead of selecting the Bullets or Numbering icons on the Home tab of Word, click the Multi-Level List option. It's just to the right of the Numbering icon. Better yet, click the arrow beside it to select the type of list to create. You can then choose the list you'd like to use. To indent to another head, click the Tab key. To go back a head, hold down the Shift key and click Tab ... or click the Return or Enter key.

Did you know?

To create a multi-level list easily, type a 1, a full stop, and type your first list item. Then press Enter. If you want to indent the next item one head, press the Tab key. A new level will be created automatically. Click Shift+Tab to move back out.

You know how to copy and paste text. You right-click the selected text, click Copy, and then, with the mouse repositioned where you want the text to be placed, right-click and select Paste. You may also know that this technique works for other data too; for instance, you can right-click a picture, click Copy, and then paste that image somewhere else. But this technique does not work if you want to copy *only* the formatting you've applied to text. Formatting can include font colour, size, or type, underline, bold, or italic, or even text effects, highlighting and similar options.

If you've applied formatting to a particular portion of a document and you want to copy that formatting and apply it to another part of the document, use the Format Painter. It does just what you'd expect; it applies formatting you've copied.

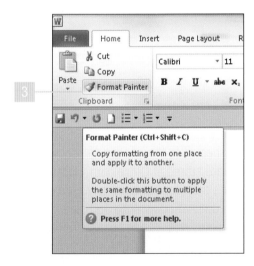

Use the Format Painter

1. In Word, apply various formatting to a particular part of text.

2. Select the text.

3. From the Home screen, click Format Painter.

4. Drag the mouse, which now has a paint brush beside the cursor, over the text to apply the formatting to.

4

Did you know?

If you decide not to apply formatting using Format Painter after clicking the Format Painter button, click with the mouse once to cancel.

Explore templates

Before we get too much further in to using Microsoft Office Word, you should really take a few moments to explore the templates available to you. While you could create all your documents from scratch, there's no need to reinvent the wheel every time you need to do something. Word offers templates that are ready to be personalised, and they are available from the File tab. You can use these templates to create award certificates, brochures, Get Well cards, and even CVs, while only investing a few minutes to personalise them to meet your needs.

You have to be connected to the internet to access most of the templates, as they are stored at Office.com. Because they are stored 'in the cloud', they don't take up any hard drive space on your computer (until you download and save them) and Microsoft and template creators can change, update, or add more templates easily. Templates come with themes, colours fonts and font sizes already built-in, applied and configured. All you have to do is highlight the text to change, insert a picture (if desired), and save the resulting file to your computer.

It's important to note that Microsoft can, at any time, remove templates, replace them with others, re-categorise them or move them to another folder. It might be best then, when you're looking for a specific template, to search for it. There's a window that's available just for that purpose. This also means that any template you see used in this book may or may not be available to you; it could have been deleted from the templates library.

If you want, you can get templates from http://office.microsoft.com instead of from the File tab in Word. From there you can browse templates, and if you find one you like, you can download it directly. As with any download, simply opt to save the file to your hard drive, and when ready, open it in Word.

Did you know?

You can create your own templates and submit them to Microsoft. You never know, one just may make the cut!

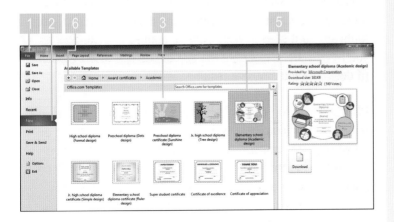

Browse available templates

1 In Word, click the File tab.

2 Click New.

3 Under the Office.com section, browse the available template categories.

4 Double-click any category and note the subcategories.

5 Click any template once to preview it in the right pane.

6 Click the Back button to return to the main categories.

4

Explore templates (cont.)

Important

If you're looking for something specific, type a keyword into the Search box and click the arrow to see what's available.

Create an award certificate

1. In Word, click File and New.

2. Click Award Certificates.

3. Note the Award Certificate categories, explore them, and decide on a certificate.

4. Click it to download it.

5. Use what you know about text editing to type the required information into the certificate.

6. Save or print the certificate as applicable.

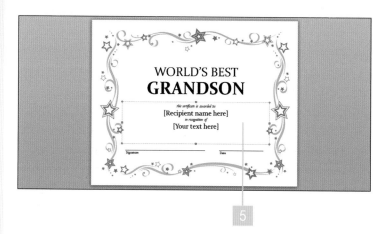

Create a flyer, brochure or for sale sign

Introduction

When you need to quickly create a document such as a For Sale sign or a flyer for a lost pet, you can do so in Word. You can also create more complex documents including brochures, newsletters and invitations. You can create these items from scratch or you can search for a related template you can edit, a skill you explored briefly at the end of the last chapter. If you know what kind of document you want to create, it only takes a minute or so to search the templates for a starting place; if you don't find what you want, you can always start from a blank page.

Whatever you decide to create, you'll likely need to input text, pictures and perhaps clip art. You may need to create a table to organise your data in columns or rows. You will probably need to resize the images you insert, and wrap text around them. You may even want to add a border, apply a background, or insert a 'drop cap'. When you incorporate these things you enhance the document; you draw attention to it.

While we can't tell you how to create the perfect document, we can tell you that the goal is to have people take notice of your work and be able to discern its meaning quickly (you're searching for a lost dog, for instance, or you have a boat to sell). To be successful, you have to add just the right amount of elements; you can't add so many that you distract from the idea you're conveying, but you want your audience to sit up and take notice too. Much of the time, simple words on a page won't grab a reader's attention.

What you'll do

Position text on the page

Position images on the page

Add borders and backgrounds

In this chapter you'll learn the skills required to add elements. You'll learn to align text, create columns of text, and wrap text around an image. You'll learn to resize images and edit them (although most editing should be done prior to inserting the picture in Word), and apply a page border and background. You'll even learn how to start a brochure with a drop cap!

?

Did you know?

There are several ways in which you can format a 'heading'. Here, from the Home screen, we started with 'Normal' text, added bold and underlining from the Font group, changed the font to Broadway, changed the font size to 36 and then clicked the Center button on the Paragraph group.

?

Did you know?

You can choose any of the style sets shown here to access additional styles. Try Elegant, Modern, Fancy and Formal. You can probably apply these styles to create home-made wedding invitations (or at least give your wedding planner an idea of what your daughter and son-in-law-to-be are looking for).

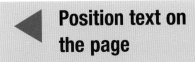

Very rarely do you simply start typing and stop when you're finished, leaving everything as one long paragraph or a series of them. Most of the time, especially with flyers, brochures and For Sale signs, you position the text so that it's easier to read and so that the reader can make out, very quickly, what the document is trying to convey. In the case of a For Sale sign or a sign for a lost pet, you'd likely 'centre' large text across the top of the document, as below. Notice that the formatting button 'Center' is selected, hence, the centring of the text in the heading.

If you'd rather not spend your limited time formatting your own heading, you can opt for one of the preconfigured styles. This is the Title style from the Default (Black and White) Style Set, available from the Home tab and the Styles group. You could easily centre this if desired by clicking the Center button instead of the Align Left option chosen here.

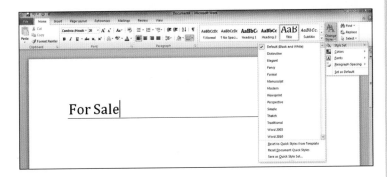

5

Position text on the page (cont.)

Input and align text

1 Type a heading in Word. Try For Sale, Lost Dog or something similar.

2 Verify the cursor is still positioned on the line of text. To be sure, place the cursor between For and Sale, or Lost and Dog.

3 From the Home tab, in the Paragraph group, click or hover the mouse over each alignment option:

a Align Text Left – this setting is the default. Text is positioned to the left of the page.

b Center – this setting positions the text in the centre of the line.

c Align Text Right – this setting positions the text to the far right of the page. As you type, the text moves to the left (from the right).

d Justify – this setting aligns text to both the left and the right margins, adding extra space as necessary to keep the text aligned.

Did you know?

The best way to see how Justify works is to type a paragraph, select the entire thing, then click the Justify button. (Click it again to remove the alignment.) You'll see how clean the paragraph looks with even spacing on each line.

There are lots of ways to create columns of text. You can use tab stops and set margins to enter some data, especially data that only consists of short words or phrases. This is an easy way to organise data in a table-like list without actually creating a table. All you have to do here is type the first entry for the first column, click the Tab key and type the next. This doesn't work very well for data that isn't a list, though; it isn't a good option when you have paragraphs to write, such as in a newsletter.

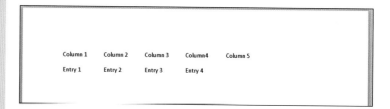

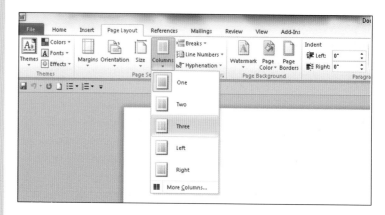

You can also create columns from the Page Layout tab. There's a Column option in the Page Setup group. You can create the text first, select it and then apply it in columns. Or you can create columns prior to typing the data. Once the columns have been configured, you can add a vertical line between them by clicking Columns again, clicking More Columns and then selecting the Line between check box. You can also adjust the column width and spacing.

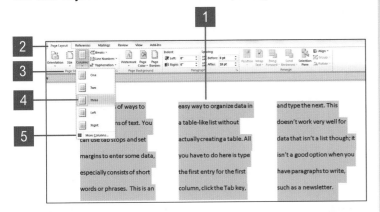

Did you know?

You can change the layout from a one-column to a two-column layout, and then you can change back to the single-column layout on a later page.

Important

It's always seemed easier for us to type the text first and then apply columns.

You can create columns of text in other ways too. You may prefer to create a table; tables are excellent choices if you're creating columns for a web page, a professional printer or just because you prefer it! Tables keep their shape, so to speak, and rarely cause problems when transferred to other mediums, like the Internet. You learned to create a simple table in Chapter 2.

Create columns of text

1 Select the text you want formatted in columns, or place your cursor where you want columns to begin.

2 Click the Page Layout tab.

3 In the Page Setup group, click Columns.

4 To apply columns quickly, select how many columns you want.

5 To see more options:

a Click More Columns.

b Click the number of columns that you want.

c In the Apply to list, click Selected text or This point forward.

Position text on the page (cont.)

Create a drop cap

1 Position the mouse before the first letter of a paragraph, preferably the first paragraph on the page.

2 Click the Insert tab.

3 Click Drop Cap.

4 From the drop-down list, click Dropped.

Finally, if you're going to create a newsletter, flyer, For Sale sign or something similar, consider using a template. Templates already have preconfigured columns and elements, and are often professionally designed. This means that you don't have to worry so much about formatting, the number of elements you use, backgrounds, borders or even where images should be inserted. It's all done for you!

To 'cap' off your creation, consider adding a drop cap. Drop caps look great on newsletters and brochures and draw the reader's attention easily. Drop caps are simple to create; just select the letter and add the drop cap formatting.

Chapter 5

Create a Flyer, Brochure, or For Sale Sign

When you need to quickly create a document such as a For Sale sign or a flyer for a lost pet, you can do so in Word. You can also create more complex documents including brochures, newsletters, and the like. You can create these items from scratch or you can search for a related template you can edit, a skill you explored briefly at the end of the last chapter. If you know what kind of document you want to create, it only takes a minute or so to search the templates for a starting place; if you don't find what you want, you can always start from a blank page.

1

Add a picture to a page and you'll inevitably have to edit it, at least somewhat. You may need to resize it, move it, add a border, or even change its brightness or contrast. Much of this is lessened when you use a template; templates have 'image placeholders', and when you swap out your image for the one in the template, it often fits inside the space exactly as it should. This doesn't make your picture any better, mind you, but it does generally eliminate the need to resize and reposition it.

Take a look at this flyer. It's a template we found under Flyers, Real Estate under File, New. Notice that it's simple to right-click the image placeholder and change the picture. If you are selling your home, you could use this flyer as a base, take a picture of the front of your house and switch it for this one. If you're an agent, you could even keep the 'Local Sales Agent' part of the flyer and replace the information there with your own (including your own professional picture). Your pictures should be automatically resized to fit in the space provided.

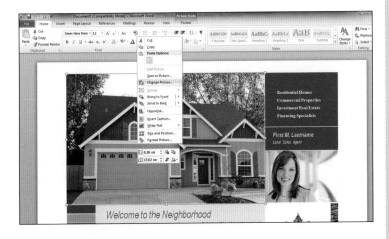

You can't always find a flyer you want to use, though. Often, especially in the case of a For Sale sign or Cake Sale flyer (or the like), you don't need to anyway. You simply need to create a heading, type the date and time, and insert a picture. With the picture inserted, you resize and position it to suit your needs.

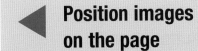

Position images on the page

5

Position images on the page (cont.)

Resize an image

1. Insert an image into a document.
2. Select the image.
3. Use the alignment options on the Home tab (Paragraph group), to align the image.
4. Position the cursor at any corner of the image.
5. Click and drag to resize it.

Wrap text around a picture or clip art

1. Insert at least a paragraph of text.
2. Insert a picture.
3. Click the picture to select it.
4. Click the Picture Tools tab.
5. Click Position and hover over the various options to preview them.
6. Click Wrap Text and hover over the various options to preview them.
7. Click any option to apply it.

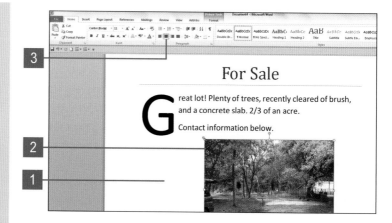

If your needs are a little more complex, say you're creating a newsletter and want to position the text so that it wraps around a picture, you can do that too. It's easiest to write the text, insert the picture, size it appropriately and then try the formatting options for wrapping and positioning text. The options are available from the Page Layout tab and only become visible when the picture is selected.

You'll explore two options from the Page Layout tab with a picture selected in a document that also contains text: Position and Wrap Text. As you explore the options you can preview how it'll look if you apply it. Instead of naming and detailing each option, it's best if you simply explore the options.

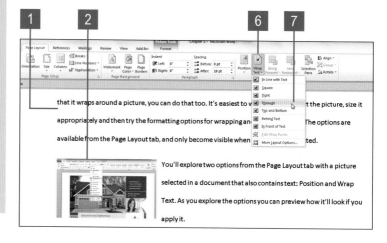

You probably would not add borders and backgrounds to a letter you've written to a doctor or lawyer. There's no need. Professionals who get letters in the post will generally read them, regardless of how eye-catching they are (or are not). Besides, backgrounds can be distracting and printing them requires you use a lot more ink than if you did not. However, if you're trying to get someone to read a flyer you've created, to enhance a family newsletter, to get someone to attend a play, cake sale or golf tournament, or to rent your upstairs apartment, you will need to add some flair. That's where backgrounds and borders come in.

You know that most templates are preconfigured with backgrounds and borders, among other things. If you can find a template you like and can use it as a basis for your creation, that's the way to go. As you can see here, templates come in all flavours. If you can't find a template you like, you can add your own borders and backgrounds. You add page borders and backgrounds from the Page Layout tab.

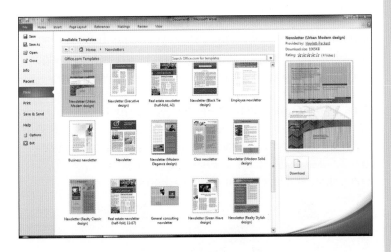

Let's start with a blank page and page borders. Page borders can add elegance to a formal invitation, help frame a flyer or newsletter, or draw the reader's eyes to the document if it's posted on a bulletin board, sign or lamp post. You create your page border from the Page Layout tab, by clicking Page Borders.

5

Add borders and backgrounds (cont.)

Add a page border

1. In any document, click the Page Layout tab.

2. Click Page Borders.

3. Apply border options as desired.

4. To apply the options you've selected, click OK.

Important

When you print documents that have backgrounds, you use a lot of extra ink.

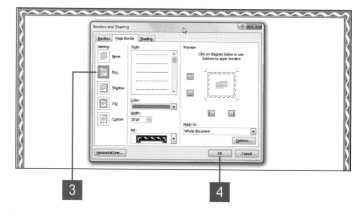

Note that you can select various kinds of borders including Box, Shadow, 3D and Custom. Each has its own settings and options. Generally, you can choose the style, colour, width and even art. Your best bet here is to experiment with these options. It's important to understand that when you choose an option from the left pane the options in the right one change. And when you choose an option on the right, they may change again! Here we've selected various options, including art.

When adding a background you can select a solid colour or, like the Page Borders options, apply your own touches. Page Color has the option to add Fill Effects, which include things like shading, textures, patterns and pictures. Here we've applied a texture and, as you can guess, pictures could prove to be a little more background than you need!

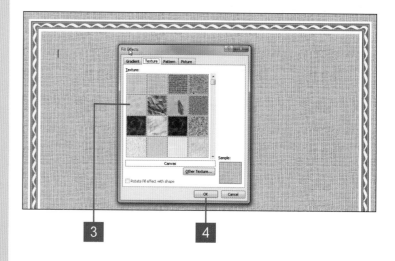

As you explore the available backgrounds and fill effects, try the following:

- Gradients – a gradient type of shading. You can incorporate two colours, if you like, and those colours will blend into each other for a nice, easy-to-view background. Gradients can be configured with a style too, including Horizontal, Vertical and more. Here, From corner is selected.

- Textures – browse the textures and select one that matches the theme of your document. There are lots of textures available, including Denim, Fish Fossil, White Marble, Parchment (which might be nice for a wedding invitation) and various wood grains.

- Patterns – apply a pattern if desired. There are patterns that contain dots, lines, squares, triangles and more. Be careful not to make the document background 'too busy' or it will distract from the document's purpose.

- Picture – you can select a picture to use as a background. If you use a picture and the page is longer than the picture, it will repeat as a pattern.

Apply a background to a page

1. In any document, click the Page Layout tab.

2. Click Page Color.

3. Select a solid colour to serve as the background, if desired.

4. To add fill effects:

   a. Click Page Colour.

   b. Click Fill Effects.

   c. Explore each tab, selecting options as desired.

   d. Refer to the sample box to see how the changes will look on the page.

   e. Click OK.

5

Create a booklet, newsletter or novel

Introduction

Now you're ready to create something big, and rest assured, Microsoft Word can handle it! You can use Microsoft Word to write that novel you've been trying to get to. You can create a booklet for the local community centre's lunch and activities programme. You can create the most awesome newsletter ever written. All you have to do is put down the words (perhaps via a template), format them (perhaps using columns, headings, tables and styles), add pictures or clip art, then finalise it by adding a few special elements like headers and footers or a Table of Contents.

In this chapter you'll learn how to apply these finishing touches. You'll learn how to insert a date and time for a newsletter (or perhaps a blog), how to insert special characters, and how to input page numbers, create headers and footers (for the publisher), and how to create a Table of Contents. While you learn to do these things you'll also learn how to access other features. For instance, you'll use the References tab to access Options to insert a Table of Contents, but from that same tab you can insert a citation to a book, article or periodical, add a bibliography or even insert an index (although we don't have the space to cover these things here).

What you'll do

Insert a date and time

Input special text and data

Insert additional pages

Number pages

Create headers and footers

Create a Table of Contents

Insert a date and time

Insert a static date

1 Place the cursor in the document where you'd like to insert the date.

2 Type the first few letters of the date.

3 When prompted, click Enter to accept the suggestion.

See also

You can also insert a date so that it appears in the document's header. You'll learn about adding headers and footers later in this chapter.

You may need to insert the date (and possibly even the time) in various letters, newsletters, booklets or other documents. You can manually type the date and time, or you can insert them using the Insert tab. If you opt to input the date manually by typing it, Word will try to help by suggesting the current date. If you like what you see, you simply press Enter on the keyboard. You don't have to type the entire thing. If you don't like what you see you can continue typing, inputting whatever you want, however you want, bypassing the suggestion altogether. If you'd like to accept the default offered, but it's not in the correct format, you can change that format from the Insert tab, detailed next.

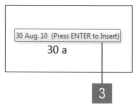

If you'd like to insert the date and time from the Insert tab, you can. While you may not feel any particular need to learn another new command, there are advantages to this method. First, you can choose any available format. Second, you can set any format as the default, so the next time you type a date, it'll appear in the format you prefer. And third, you can tell Word when you insert a date and time that you want the inserted date and time to be updated each time you open the document. This offers lots of advantages; for one, it allows you to write one form letter (for instance), input a date and then never have to fool around with that date again! The next time you open the letter to edit it, the new day's date will be automatically inserted, replacing the old date. Additionally, the automatic updating of the date and time can help you keep track of when you last edited the document.

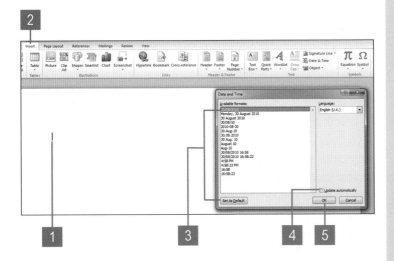

Insert a date and
time (cont.)

Insert the date and time using the Insert tab

1 Place the cursor in the document where you'd like the date or time to appear.

2 Click the Insert tab and click Date and Time.

3 If you'd like to set any format as the default, click it and then click Set As Default. Click Yes when prompted.

4 If you'd like the date or time to update automatically, click Update automatically.

5 Click OK.

Important

Sometimes you'll have to press the Enter key to insert part of the date and then press the Space key to continue. After pressing the Space key you may be further prompted to insert the rest of the date, in which case you can then press the Enter key again.

Monday (Press ENTER to Insert)
30 Mond

Input special text and data

There will be times when you need to input special characters. You may need to insert a dollar sign, ampersand, Latin or Greek letters, or a copyright symbol. You may also need to insert characters related to proofing, such as an em dash, em space, paragraph mark or similar markings. You do this from the Insert tab's Symbol option.

If you use a special character often, say you input the dollar sign quite a bit because you work with people in the United States, you can even create a shortcut key for it. We've assigned the key F10 to the dollar sign, so that when we need to input it, we simply press this key. You may want to do the same with a character you use often.

You can also create your own, personalised entries in AutoCorrect, so that when you type a specific key combination, a specific character is inserted. For instance, if you insert a plus-minus sign a lot, you can create a key combination for it, perhaps PLM followed by a space. When you do this, you never have to take your hands off the keyboard to insert the character.

You'll find all of the options from the Insert tab, under Symbol. While you can insert a commonly used symbol from the drop-down list, to access all symbols you have to click More Symbols.

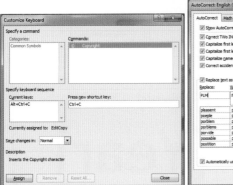

If you want to assign a shortcut key for any symbol or character, in the Symbol dialogue box, click Shortcut Key. Press the shortcut key to use, such as F10, F9, or even Ctrl+<any letter>. You can't just pick any key or key combination, though. You can't use the Windows key, Shift + a letter, or any other keys or combinations that are already spoken for. You can use the Function keys, and various versions of Ctrl + something. Don't worry, if the key combination can't be used, it won't be inserted. Click Assign and then Close when finished.

Likewise, you can assign an AutoCorrect entry. Just click AutoCorrect and configure the entry. You might use PLM for the Plus/Minus key, as noted earlier, for instance. Type the desired letters, click Add and then click OK.

Insert a special character

1 Place your cursor in the document where you'd like to insert the special character.

2 Click the Insert tab.

3 Click Symbol.

4 If you see the symbol to insert, click it.

5 If you do not see the symbol to insert:

   a Click More Symbols.

   b Under the Symbols tab, if applicable, select a Font group.

   c Under the Symbols tab, explore and select a Subset.

   d Locate the symbol to insert and click Insert.

6 To insert a special character, click the Special Characters tab. (Select the item to insert and click Insert.)

7 When you're ready to close the dialogue box, click Close (or Cancel if you did not insert any character).

Insert additional pages

You can insert additional pages if you have a multi-page document. You can insert a Cover Page to appear at the beginning of the document, a blank page anywhere in the document, or a page break to prepare a document for printing or viewing. As you'd expect, to insert one of these items, you need to use the Insert tab.

The Cover Page option from the Insert tab is a great way to introduce a novel or proposal. We suppose one could be tweaked to work for a Fax cover sheet too, but most of the options are best applied to longer documents like business proposals, yearly reports and presentations. Here you can see the Cover Page options from the Insert tab, followed by how the selected Cover Page looks once opened. This makes creating a cover sheet a breeze, because you're prompted for the necessary information and don't have to come up with it on your own. In this case, you're prompted for the type of document (perhaps a Year-End Sales Report), the year, a subtitle and a brief description. Formatting is already applied.

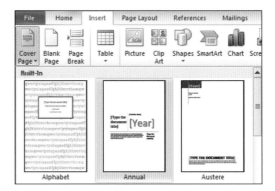

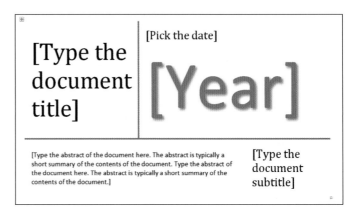

You can also input a blank page. If you're writing a novel and decide to end one chapter and start another after proofreading it a few times, you can easily do that by inserting a blank page. If you are creating a presentation and handouts, you can insert a blank page for note-taking. There are lots of reasons for inserting a blank page and it's very easy to do.

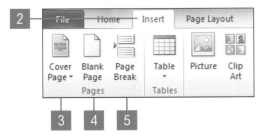

Finally, you can insert a Page Break. This moves your cursor to the beginning of the next page and allows you to create good-looking prints by telling the printer when to start a new page. This enables you to section off your data without having to hit the Return or Enter key on the keyboard multiple times until you reach the next page. Additionally, if you're using a view other than one that shows the page breaks, you can effectively enter page breaks without mess or fuss! We prefer viewing the pages breaks, but there are lots of reasons for changing that view, including viewing pages in Web Layout.

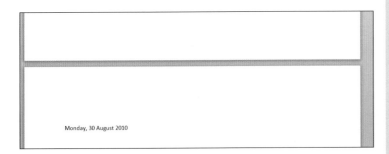

Monday, 30 August 2010

Did you know?

You can insert common equations from the Insert tab. Just click Equations and pick the one you want.

Insert additional pages

1 Place the cursor in the appropriate place on the page:

 a If inserting a Page Break, place it after the end of a paragraph or entry.

 b If inserting a blank page, place the cursor where you'd like the blank page to start.

2 Click the Insert tab.

3 To insert a Cover Page:

 a Click Cover Page.

 b Make a selection.

4 To insert a blank page, click Blank Page.

5 To insert a Page Break, click Page Break.

Number pages

When creating a long document such as a booklet, proposal, presentation, novel, etc., consider adding page numbers. Page numbers help you and your audience to keep track of the pages they're reading. You can use page numbers in combination with a Table of Contents to make data easy to find too. You add page numbers from the Insert tab. From there you can:

- Place page numbers at the top, bottom or in the margins of pages.
- Format page numbers.
- Remove page numbers.

Before you assign page numbers, take a look at the formatting options. Generally you'll want to accept the default, adding simple page numbers to pages. There are other options, though, such as adding a negative sign before page numbers, using page numbers that are Roman numerals or using letters to number pages. If you have chapter numbers, you can add those in too. To see the options, click the Insert tab, click Page Number and click Format Page Numbers.

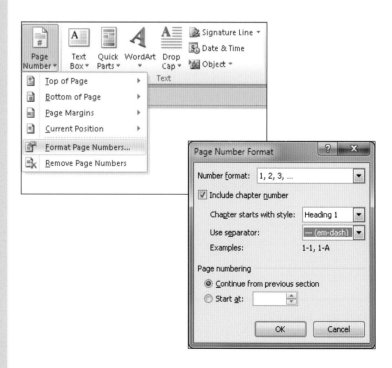

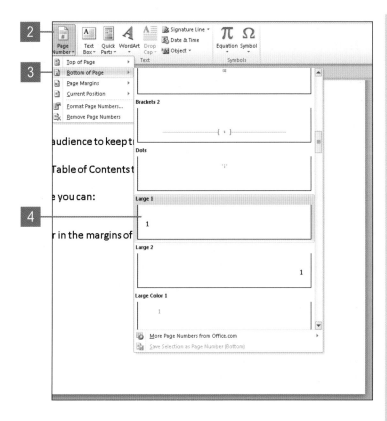

Add page numbers

1 Click the Insert tab.

2 Click Page Number.

3 Select a location.

4 Select a page number type.

5 Note the new page number in the header or footer.

6 Double-click in the document to return to the body.

Important

If you decide you don't want page numbers or do not like the style you selected, click the Insert tab and click Remove Page Numbers.

Create headers and footers

Headers and footers are additional information you can add to a document and often consist of the document title and page number. Headers appear at the top of the page and footers appear at the bottom. They appear in the margins (so they do not take up any of the typing area) and can be printed if you think they should be.

Headers and footers, while often only text, can also include graphics, paragraphs and various fields. You can add different headers and footers to odd and even pages, or use a different header or footer for a specific page or section in a document. Headers and Footers are added from the Insert tab.

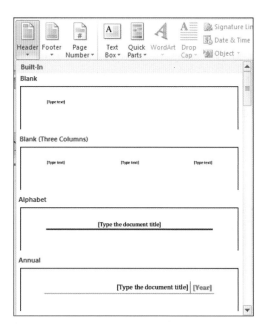

You type and format text for headers and footers in the same way that you input text in a document; you simply type what you want to include. However, there are a multitude of adjustments you can make to headers and footers, including, but not limited to, positioning them, adjusting their default tab stops, using specific headers and footers for specific sections of a document, and more. We'll just cover adding simple headers and footers here, though. If you want to learn more, refer to Word's Help feature.

Create headers and footers (cont.)

6

Add simple headers and footers

1 Click the Insert tab.

2 Click Header.

3 Select a header.

4 Type to insert the header information.

5 Repeat these steps with the footer options.

See also

When working in the header or footer, notice the new tab at the top of the page entitled Header and Footer Tools. You can use these tools to enhance the header and footer by changing the margin size, adding a page number, assigning the header or footer to only odd or even pages, and more.

Important

To exit the header and footer view, double-click anywhere in the document, or, from the Header and Footer Tools tab, click Close Header and Footer.

Create a Table of Contents

Since we've been talking about longer documents in this entire chapter, it's only appropriate that we discuss adding a Table of Contents. To have a workable Table of Contents, though, you need to have applied some formatting in the form of headings. This becomes clear when you click the Table of Contents option under the References tab. Your options include how many headings to consider. Word has to have some information about the layout of your document before it can create a Table of Contents, and cannot create a Table of Contents if your document consists only of text in the form of paragraphs.

Add a Table of Contents

1. Place the cursor where you'd like the Table of Contents to appear.
2. Click the References tab.
3. Click Table of Contents.
4. Select any option.

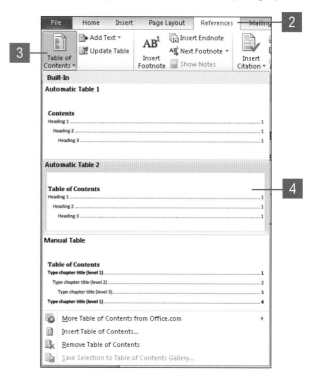

If you've assigned at least Heading 1s, you're off to a good start. If you've assigned Heading 2s, that's even better. If Word can't find these things, it'll let you know with a prompt, and if you click OK, you'll get a Table of Contents that looks like this:

> ## Contents
> No table of contents entries found.

If you do have Headings in your document, you'll be able to create a great-looking Table of Contents easily and quickly. In two clicks we created what you see below. The Table of Contents won't be automatically inserted at the beginning of the document, though; it will be inserted just after the position of your cursor. So, before you start, place the cursor in the document where you'd like to add the Table of Contents.

5 If the Table of Contents is not what you want:

a Click the Table of Contents.

b Locate the menu shown here.

c Click Remove Table of Contents.

Contents

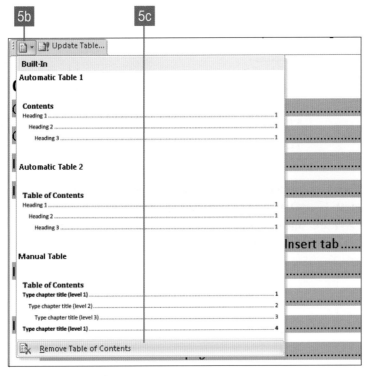

5b 5c

Update Table...

Built-In

Automatic Table 1

Contents

Heading 1 1

    Heading 2 1

        Heading 3 1

Automatic Table 2

Table of Contents

Heading 1 1

    Heading 2 1

        Heading 3 1

Insert tab......

Manual Table

Table of Contents

Type chapter title (level 1) 1

    Type chapter title (level 2) 2

        Type chapter title (level 3) 3

Type chapter title (level 1) 4

Remove Table of Contents

Share, blog and print

Introduction

Although you learned quite a bit about printing and sharing in Chapter 3, it was pretty generic. You learned how to save a file as a PDF, how to email and print a file, and how to access additional save and send options – all of which could be applied to almost any program. There are some things that are specific to Word though (or best done using Word) that were not introduced, like printing labels and envelopes, saving a blog post to the web, storing and sharing files you create in Word on Internet web servers, and similar tasks. These are the types of tasks you'll learn here.

Share via the Internet

You know enough about the Internet to know that you can find just about anything there. You can type a question and find an answer. You can look up old friends. You can pay bills, check your investments and find out what your family members are doing at any given moment. You may *not* know that you can save files to the Internet for safekeeping, though, or that it's pretty easy to create a 'blog' and post your ideas there. And you likely didn't know you can do the latter two things from the File tab of Word!

Jargon buster

Blog: A means of sharing your thoughts with the world (or only specific people) in a type of online diary. Blog is short for Web Log.

You have lots of options if you'd like to save documents to the Internet or post your thoughts and ideas to a blog; there are lots of companies that offer this. However, if you'd like to save files or post to a blog using Word and you want to do it for free, your options are much more limited.

For starters, you have to choose a *host* that offers access to web *servers* that play well with Microsoft Word. A host is generally a company that offers specific services, like access to web servers you can save your files to, save a blog to or access email from. Hosts should back up their data regularly, have tons of security features in place to keep your data safe, and be proven and reliable. You should not have to pay for a service either, and rest assured, there are lots of services that you have to pay for! Windows Live is free, offered by Microsoft, reliable, and works with Microsoft Word, and is thus the best way to go.

Jargon buster

Server: For our purposes, a server is a computer that stores files and offers access to them when you need them. Servers are backed up regularly and are secured redundantly to keep your data safe.

Host: In this instance, the entity that offers web space for storing files and a place to save and post to a blog. Hosts offer you server space.

Windows Live is a group of programs and services that is, available free from Microsoft. A Windows Live Account is a free email address you get from Microsoft for using Windows Live services. You don't have to use the account for anything other than logging in to your desired services, though; you don't have to use it as your primary or even secondary email address, although you can. You do need it to blog from Word, or to save files to the web from Word.

Choose a host for saving and blogging

7

Did you know?

When you sign up for Windows Live you get lots of perks. You get free space on the web for saving and sharing your files (which you can then access from anywhere), you get a free place to blog and you get your own, free web page that you can personalise (among other things).

Choose a host for saving and blogging (cont.)

To get a free Windows Live Account visit http://explore.live.com. Once you've created this account you'll be ready to save documents right from Word to the Internet. Just click Sign In and you'll be prompted to create an account.

Jargon buster

Windows Live – a free service from Microsoft that allows you to create, personalise and manage a small, personal, website on the World Wide Web for the purpose of storing, backing up, accessing and sharing documents, music, videos and pictures, as well as staying in touch with others.

There are several reasons you should learn how to save your documents *to the Internet*. Imagine what would happen if your home caught fire or flooded. Your computer would be destroyed, as would your backups. It doesn't matter if those backups are on CDs, DVDs, or external backup devices; if there's a fire or flood, it's likely all going to be destroyed, unless you've saved your data somewhere else (like on the Internet).

When you save important data to a web server you access from the Internet, it's 'in the cloud'. That web server may be in a nearby city, a nearby country, or halfway across the world. If something happens to your computer, you can go to the library, a friend's house, or use any available computer with Internet access to log on to your personalised web space and retrieve your important data. Not only that, though, you can share that data with your children, friends or co-workers, as applicable.

Important

Save your will, medical directives, prescription information, power of attorneys and such to an online web server, add your children to the list of those who can access these documents, and no matter where they are or where you are, those documents will always be available.

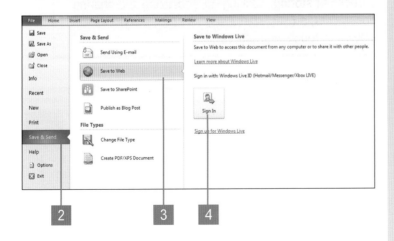

Save a file to the web

1 In Word, with a document open, click the File tab.

2 Click Save & Send.

3 Click Save to Web.

4 Click Sign In.

5 Type your Windows Live ID and password. Click OK.

7

Save to the web (cont.)

6 Select the folder where the file should be saved.

7 Name the file and click Save.

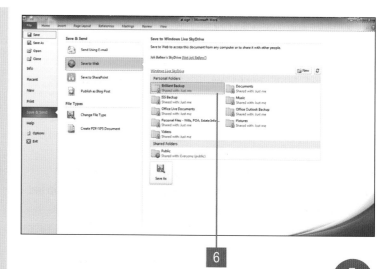

6

See also

If you haven't considered Windows Live Essentials, which are programs including Windows Live Photo Gallery, Windows Live Messenger, visit www.live.com to learn more.

For your information

You can access the file from any computer with Internet access by going to www.live.com, logging in, and clicking Office and Recent documents. Alternatively, you can click Windows Live and then SkyDrive. SkyDrive is shown here.

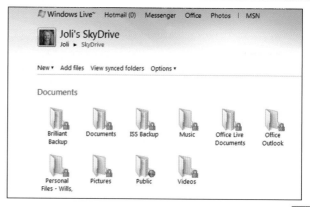

See also

Spend some time personalising your own, personalised web space on the Internet at www.live.com. Your Windows Live web page, which is free and configured automatically, offers a place to create a personal profile, a folder for uploading pictures, email access and more.

You already know that a blog is a 'web log', and is often an online journal or diary. Most people blog daily, and post their thoughts on topics like religion, politics, personal observations, family news, weather and the like. You may prefer to blog about your children or grandchildren, community centre events, or even the progress of a friend's recovery from an accident or illness.

To blog, you have to have a blogging service set up, but Windows Live, in particular Windows Live Spaces, is supported. You can create a blog post in Word and post it to your own personal blog quickly and easily, right from the File tab.

To get started, visit http://spaces.live.com. Create your blog space. Once created you can view your space, write a blog entry, customise your space and more. After setting up your space, write down your space name and secret word.

Did you know?

In Word, from the File tab, click New. There you can select Blog post, if desired, and create a blog post using a template.

Post to a blog

7

Post to a blog (cont.)

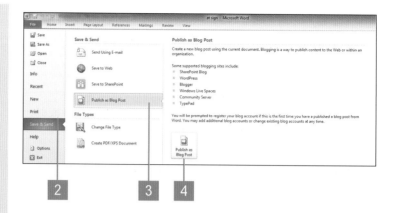

Create and post to a blog

1 In Word, with a document to post open, click the File menu.

2 Click Save & Send.

3 Click Publish as a blog post. Note the supported blog services.

4 Click Publish as a blog post in the right pane.

5 Follow all prompts to register, choosing Windows Live Spaces as the Blog provider.

6 If you need help registering your Windows Live Space, click Show Me How. However, if you've written down your space name and secret word, registration should be pretty easy.

7 Type a title if you have not done so, and complete the blog post entry.

8 From the Blog Post tab, click Publish and click Publish again.

9 You can now close Word.

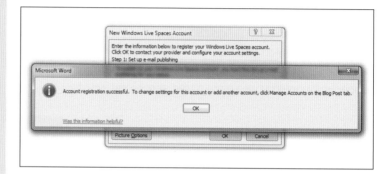

Important

If you don't type a title for the post, you'll get an error message and the post won't be published.

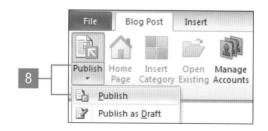

You know how to print documents, presentations, letters and other types of files. You click the File tab and click Print. If you've personalised the Quick Access toolbar or the Ribbon, you may only need to click a single 'printer' icon. Not all documents are so straightforward though. For instance, printing a sheet of labels, printing envelopes, or printing one document several times while addressing each document to a different person (Mail Merge) is a bit more complex. However, there are times when you really do need to print a professional-looking letter or envelope, and knowing how to do that when the time comes is essential.

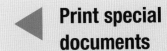

Print special documents

7

Print labels

When you think of mailing labels, you might think about a single label with a single address on it, the type of label you'd associate with a large shipping box or carton. You might think about a sheet of labels that contain your own name and address, the type of label you'd put on the return portion of an envelope. You might even think about printing a single mailing label for everyone in your address book, for the purpose of sending a mass mailing to friends and family or creating an awesome-looking (physical) address book.

There are lots of label vendors. There's Microsoft, 3M/Post-it, Ace Label, Avery, Planet, Staples and others. Each of these vendors offers various sizes and paper types. When you print labels in Word, you have to tell Word what type of label you're using. You can generally find this information on the back of the label or on the packaging. If you don't know what type of label you have, though, you may still be able to use it. As you can see here, the label sheet you have can be compared to the Details page of the Label Options dialogue box, although going this route is certainly the longest way around the task. It's better to find out the exact name and type of the labels you have before starting.

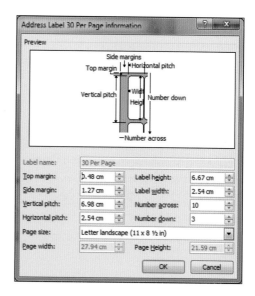

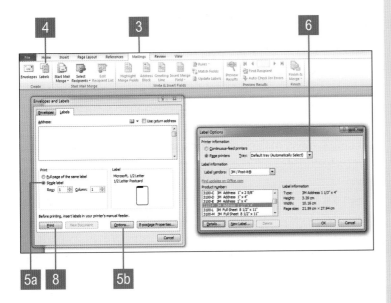

4 3 6

5a 8 5b

For your information

Right-click the address and click Font to format the text.

Did you know?

If you use Outlook and you've input names and addresses into your Contacts list, you can click the small address book icon in the Envelopes and Labels dialogue box to select the recipient from the list. This can reduce the amount of typing you have to do, but note that you may have more than one address book, which can complicate the task of finding the proper address.

Print labels (cont.)

Create a single mailing label

1 Place the label in the printer, verify the printer is connected to the computer, and turn it on as applicable.

2 Open a new document.

3 Click the Mailings tab.

4 Click Labels.

5 In the Envelopes and Labels dialogue box:

  a Click Single label.

  b Click Options.

6 From the Label Options dialog box:

  a Select your printer type.

  b Select the proper tray.

  c Select a label vendor.

  d Select a product number.

  e If you'd like to, click Details to verify you've selected the proper label.

  f Click OK.

7 Back at the Envelopes and Labels dialogue box, type the address.

8 Click Print.

Print labels (cont.)

Create a sheet of return mailing labels

1 Place the label sheet in the printer, verify the printer is connected to the computer, and turn it on as applicable.

2 Open a new document.

3 Click the Mailings tab.

4 Click Labels.

5 In the Envelopes and Labels dialogue box:

 a Click Full page of the same label.

 b Click Options.

6 From the Label Options dialogue box:

 c Select your printer type.

 d Select the proper tray.

 e Select a label vendor.

 f Select a product number.

 g If you'd like to, click Details to verify you've selected the proper label.

 h Click OK.

7 Back at the Envelopes and Labels dialogue box, type the address. (Remember you can right-click the address and click Font to format the text.)

8 Click Print.

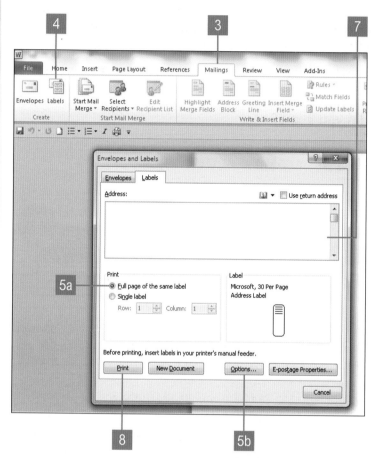

If you know how to print labels and you have labels handy, you can print a label and stick it to an envelope. This might be faster than printing an envelope, especially if you're already familiar with the task of printing labels. (Of course, it's the only option if your printer doesn't accept envelopes.) If you'd rather be a bit more professional, and your printer supports it, you can print envelopes directly from Word to your printer. You may have noticed the Envelopes option next to the Labels options on the Mailings tab; that's where you'll start.

Print envelopes

Print an envelope

1 Place the envelope in the printer tray, make sure the printer is connected to the computer, and turn it on.

2 From a new document, click the Mailings tab.

3 Click Envelopes.

Did you know?

You can click Labels on the Mailings tab and then click the Envelopes tab, if you prefer.

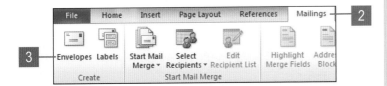

Once you've accessed the Envelopes tab, you'll see a place to type the delivery address and the return address. You can see a preview of the envelope that's selected by default, too. As with labels you can click Options to see more about the envelope selected, but here you also have the option to choose a font for both the return and delivery addresses from inside the dialogue box itself. You can even add electronic postage if you've installed the required 'electronic postage software' and signed up for any required services.

Print envelopes (cont.)

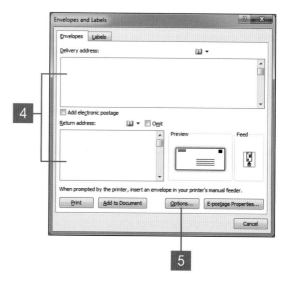

4 Type the delivery address and the return address.

5 Click Options and under the Envelope Options tab:

   a Select the envelope size.

   b Choose a delivery address font.

   c Choose a return address font.

6 Under the Printing Options tab:

   a Select a feed method.

   b Select other printing options.

   c Click OK.

7 Click Print.

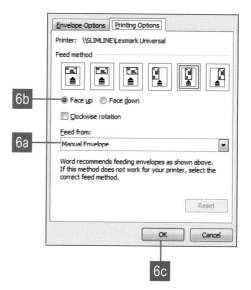

Mail Merge is a feature of Word that enables you to print documents that are similar except for unique elements such as names, addresses, phone numbers, cities, countries, etc. You could use Mail Merge to send the same letter to all of the people in your contact list, while at the same time addressing that letter directly to the intended recipient automatically. Without Mail Merge, you'd have to change the name and address on each letter manually, and print each letter one at a time. Mail Merge automates this task.

Mail Merge can also be used to personalise, address and automate the creation of email messages. It enables you to send email messages to a group of people, while personalising the email message each receives by addressing the message only to them. As you'd expect, you can also print envelopes and labels. If you want to create a mass mailing to everyone in your contact list, you can. You can even create a single document containing a catalogue or printed list of addresses.

Because there are so many options for Mail Merge, it's important to note that we could write an entire chapter on using Mail Merge to create various printouts, mailings or email messages. There's no way we can tell you how to do it all here. That said, we'll introduce the Mail Merge Wizard and we'll leave it to you to explore further, should you desire.

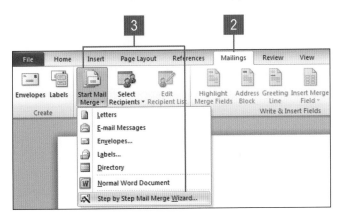

Explore the Mail Merge Wizard

Explore Mail Merge

1 Open a new Word document.

2 Click the Mailings tab.

3 Click Start Mail Merge and click Step by Step Mail Merge Wizard.

?

Did you know?

You can click and drag the Mail Merge 'window' from the right pane to anywhere in the document.

Explore the Mail Merge Wizard (cont.)

4 Select the type of document you're working on.

5 Click Next: Starting Document to continue.

6 What you see next is determined by what you selected in Step 4, thus, you'll have to make the required decisions for each part of the Wizard.

7 As you work through the Wizard, continue clicking Next until complete.

You'll eventually be prompted to select recipients. You can use an existing list you've created (which you'll browse to), you can select recipients from your Outlook contacts or you can create a brand- new list from scratch. When you do this, you'll also have to state which fields you'd like to consider, and perhaps add a greeting line, electronic postage, title, first name, last name and more. Once you've completed the Wizard, you will have the opportunity to preview your Mail Merge and print it.

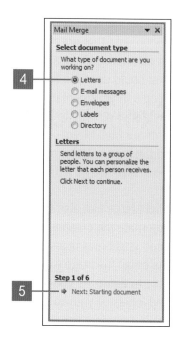

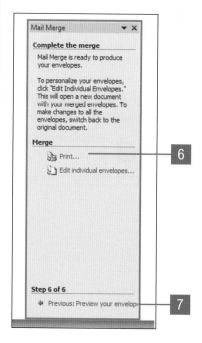

Excel basics

Introduction

Microsoft Excel is a spreadsheet program. You'll use it to keep track of data, including mathematical data that applies to investments, retirement and budgets, and also data that applies to your business such as inventories, costs and outlays. You can perform calculations on any data too. You can easily get an average of a column or row of numbers, add specific data or even calculate interest on a credit balance.

You can track and manage other types of data too; you're not relegated to money and business. You can track your weight, blood sugar or blood pressure, workout regimen and similar data. You can create a database of information that requires no calculations at all, such as an address book, complete with phone numbers, addresses, names, email addresses or any other field imaginable. You can also create forms you can print out, such as ones you might use to sell Girl Guide cookies or raffle tickets.

As with Microsoft Word and other programs, you can also work from templates. Excel's templates are, like Word's, available from the File tab. There are preconfigured templates for agendas, budgets, calendars, databases, forms, inventory lists, invoices, labels, receipts, schedules, statements and time sheets, just to name a few. We'll encourage you to use templates when applicable; there's no need to reinvent the wheel. Templates often come complete with preformatted headings, rows and columns, and include calculations that are already built-in.

What you'll do

Explore the Excel interface

Move around in a worksheet

Edit data

Format cells

Insert rows and columns

Explore templates

Explore the Excel interface

To move around in Excel you have to understand the Excel interface. If you already have experience with Microsoft Word or another Office program, you'll notice similarities. You'll see the File and Home tabs, and Insert, Page Layout and View. You'll also see tabs you've never seen before, including Formulas and Data.

The first thing you should do in Excel is click each tab to see how the Ribbon changes with the tab. The Home tab will look familiar, and offers a place to format text, set alignment options, and cut, copy and paste, and was outlined briefly in Chapters 1 and 2. However, it also has formatting options that are likely to be unfamiliar to you. For example, conditional formatting lets you apply highlighting and colour to data that meets specific requirements that you set such as data that is greater or less than a specific amount, is between two numbers, or has text that contains specific words. You can add conditional formatting to dates and duplicate values too. There are also options to merge 'cells', format a table and apply cell styles. And that's just the beginning. Click the Home tab to see the options.

See also

If you've chosen Excel as your starting point, make sure you've read the first three chapters of this book for an overview of Microsoft Office so that you can familiarise yourself with some of the basic Office principles and options.

Jargon buster

Cell – every small square you see in the body of Excel is called a cell. Cells are, in essence, Excel's 'building blocks'.

As you continue to explore the Excel interface, you'll continue to see things that are available in other Microsoft Office programs you've used (now or in the past). For instance, from the Insert tab you can insert pictures, clip art and shapes. You can insert text boxes, equations and symbols. From the Review tab you can insert comments, check spelling and use a Thesaurus. From the View tab you can change how Excel appears on the page, including options to zoom or view full screen. These are common tasks across all Office programs.

However, because Excel is unique and is used for creating and managing data spreadsheets, you'll see tasks that are unique to it as well. As an example, the Formulas tab offers access to all kinds of formulae from Financial to Maths and Trig to Statistical (under More Functions). You use Formulas to perform calculations on data. Of course, there are other tabs to explore, too; the idea is to familiarise yourself with them now, so that you can go into more depth more easily later.

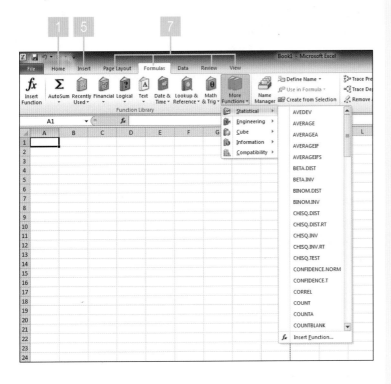

Explore the Excel interface

1. Open Excel and click the Home tab.

2. Locate the Cut, Copy and Paste commands.

3. Locate the drop-down lists for the font, font size, highlighting and text colour.

4. Explore other options in the Home tab.

5. Click the Insert tab.

6. From the Insert tab, notice you can insert pictures, clip art, shapes and similar data. Note you can also insert charts, text and symbols.

7. Continue by clicking each of the other tabs:

   a Page Layout.

   b Formulas.

   c Data.

   d Review.

   e View.

8

Move around in a worksheet

A worksheet is the page you see when you open Excel. If you look to the bottom left in the Excel window in the figure below, you'll see that there are three available worksheets, and Sheet 1 (which can be renamed) is selected. This is the default look and feel of any Excel book. If you look to the bottom right, you'll notice we've moved the Zoom slider to 150% so that the cells are easier to see. Cell A1 is selected.

Explore ways to move around in Excel

1 Place your cursor in cell A1 of a new, blank worksheet.

2 Use the Zoom slider in the bottom right corner to make the cells large enough to see comfortably.

3 Click any cell using the mouse. Try to click C3 and F8.

4 Press each of the arrow keys on the keyboard several times.

5 Click the Page Up and Page Down buttons to move up or down one 'screen length'.

6 Press the Home key on the keyboard to return quickly to cell A1.

7 Use the scroll button on your mouse to quickly scroll through rows of data.

8 Click Sheet 2 and Sheet 3 to see additional worksheets.

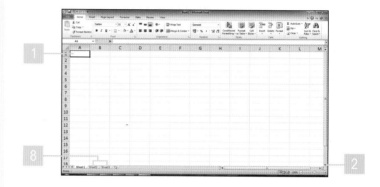

To get the most from Excel and to use it effectively, you have to become familiar with the interface, cells, tabs and such. The first step is to navigate a worksheet. You can move around in a worksheet in various ways:

▥ Click any cell using the mouse.

▥ Move from cell to cell by pressing the arrow keys on the keyboard.

▥ Use the Page Up and Page Down buttons to quickly move up or down one 'screen length'.

▥ Press the Home key on the keyboard to return quickly to cell A1.

▥ Use the scroll button on your mouse to quickly scroll through rows of data.

Did you know?

There are myriad other shortcuts beyond using the keyboard to move around in a worksheet. For instance, Ctrl+Page Up moves you to the previous worksheet in the same file, while Ctrl+Page Down moves to the next one. F1 launches the Help files. F7 launches the spell checker.

It's easy to input numbers and text into a cell; you simply click and type. Sometimes, though, you'll need to edit that data after you've input it. There are two ways to do this. You can replace everything in the cell or edit only a part of its contents. If you want to replace everything in the cell, you click the cell and start typing over it. When you edit data this way, all of the existing information in the cell is 'written over'. If you want to edit something while not deleting what's in the cell (perhaps you've misspelled a word or need to input another number in a string of numbers), you'll need to double-click first.

Here's an example of the latter. In this worksheet, we're calculating what happens if we make optional extra payments on our home loan. We initially configure it to be £200, but now we're thinking we can do £300. One way to make this change is to highlight the 2 and change it to a 3.

Loan Amortization Schedule

	Enter values
Loan amount	£ 87,500.00
Annual interest rate	5.50 %
Loan period in years	15
Number of payments per year	12
Start date of loan	12/12/2003
Optional extra payments	200

For your information

When you are finished editing, you click outside the cell to automatically recalculate, to see your changes or to otherwise apply the change.

Edit data in a cell

1 To type over what's already in a cell:

   a Click the cell.

   b Type the desired data.

   c Click outside the cell.

2 To edit what's in a cell without deleting its contents:

   a Double-click the cell.

   b Position the cursor by clicking the mouse again or use the arrow keys on the keyboard.

   c Type the desired additional data or use the Backspace or Delete key to remove data.

   d Click outside the cell.

Edit data (cont.)

There are ways to insert data while simultaneously editing it. For instance, you can insert today's date into a cell, click and drag from the bottom right corner of that cell and automatically add subsequent dates to the cells you drag your mouse over. Although you'd expect you can do this with the names of months, days of the week or days in a month, you can do the same with various other types of data that Excel recognises. Here's an example: we started with 'first quarter of 2010' and dragged the cursor downwards from the bottom right corner of that cell to add subsequent dates.

	A	B
1	1Q2010	
2	2Q2010	
3	3Q2010	
4		
5		
6		3Q2011
7		
8		
9		
10		

01:00
02:00
03:00
04:00
05:00
06:00
07:00
08:00
09:00
10:00

You know how to input data into cells; you simply click and type. You can opt to format any data before or after typing it or you can simply leave the data as-is. You don't have to format text with a font and font colour, and you don't have to add currency symbols or numbers after the decimal unless you want to. While some formatting may be necessary, much formatting is often optional.

Most of the formatting you'll do in Excel regarding the colour and size of text, or the background colour of cells, can be done from the Home tab. The easiest way to get started is to select one cell or a group of cells and then click the appropriate formatting options. We generally prefer using the Home tab to do this after we've added data because it seems like, in Excel at least, it's easier to input data first, take a look at it and then format it later.

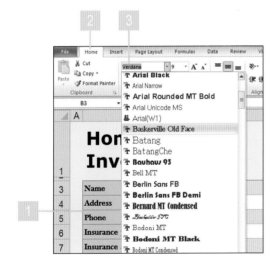

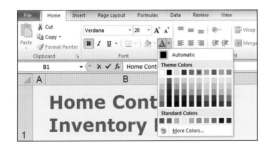

Format text in cells

1 Input and then select text. You can select a single cell, an entire row or column, or multiple rows and columns.

2 Click the Home tab.

3 From the font drop-down list, select a font. Repeat with font size.

4 With the text still selected, apply additional formatting as desired. Click:

  a **B** to bold the text.

  b *I* to italicise the text.

  c <u>U</u> to underline the text.

Important

Sometimes formatting draws your attention away from the data, when the data should be your first priority. Try adding text and cell formatting after you've input important data.

8

Format cells (cont.)

5. Click the arrow beside the Text Highlight Color icon to select a colour to highlight the text.

6. Click the arrow beside the Font Color icon to select a colour for the text.

7. Note the options in the Alignment group on the Home tab. Click any to apply.

Beyond formatting text you can also format data. You can add currency symbols, and you can tell Excel how many places after the decimal point you'd like to include with numbers, how you would like dates and time to be formatted and display and how you'd like National Insurance numbers to be displayed, among other things. You'll do most of this kind of formatting from the Format Cells dialogue box, which you can access by right-clicking any cell.

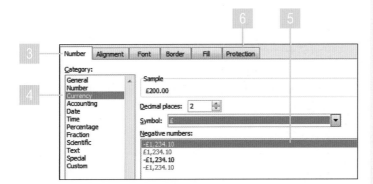

Format data in cells

1. Select any data to format. Choose a date, time, number, monetary unit, etc.

2. Right-click the selected data and click Format Cells.

3. In the Format Cells dialogue box, click the Number tab.

4. Choose the subcategory that applies to your data.

5. Select the desired formatting.

6. Note the other tabs; you use these tabs to apply additional formatting.

7. Click OK.

For your information

Notice when you select and right-click cells that the mini toolbar appears where you can quickly add popular formatting options like bold, italic, highlighting, text colour, and font type and size.

Finally, you can format data and cells by adding a 'fill color', aligning the text in the cell to the left, centre right, top, bottom, and other areas of the cell, you can wrap text so it'll fit in a cell and more. You can even add a pattern style or pattern colour, although we believe this type of formatting draws attention away from the important data you're keeping or conveying. When you applied formatting to numbered data using the Format Cells dialogue box's Number tab, you may have noticed the additional tabs:

- Alignment – to assign text alignment options including Wrap text, Shrink to fit, and to tell Excel where in the cell to place data (to the right, left, top, bottom, etc.).

- Font – to select a font, font style, font size, font colour and to add effects such as strikethough.

Format cells
(cont.)

Format the entire spreadsheet

1 Click the cell in the top right corner of the worksheet. It's the cell with the triangle in it.

2 With the entire worksheet selected, click the Ctrl key on the keyboard, hold it down, and click 1.

3 From the Format Cells dialogue box, apply formatting as desired.

Did you know?

You can open the Format Cells dialogue box by using the key combination Ctrl+1.

Border – to show or hide borders in cells. You can also apply a border colour.

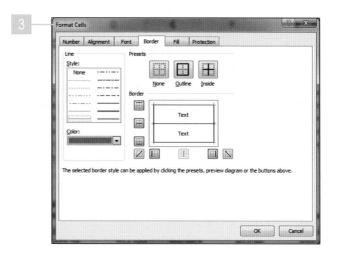

Fill – to add a background (or fill) colour to cells. You can also apply a pattern and pattern colour.

Protection – to protect cells or hide formulas, to be used in conjunction with the Protect Sheet button available from the Review tab).

See also

You can apply formatting from the Home tab after selecting data already entered as an option for formatting text in Word, PowerPoint and Outlook, as formatting does not change that much from program to program.

You may, at some point, want to apply specific formatting to the entire worksheet. You may want to format the entire worksheet with a specific font, fill colour, border and the like, for instance. You'll perform the task of formatting the usual way, from the Format Cells dialogue box. But first, you'll need to select the entire worksheet.

Often you'll need to insert a row or a column after adding data. This happens regularly, so Excel has made it easy to make adjustments when necessary. Here's an example of a personal budget worksheet. Note the options under Entertainment include Cable TV, Video/DVD rentals, Movies/plays and Concerts/clubs. However, if golf is one of your major entertainment expenditures, and if you can't simply edit an existing row, you'll need to add a new one. You may have to add several! (Boating, Rowing, Fishing, Drinking, for example.)

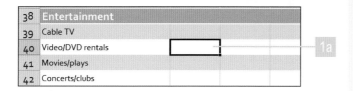

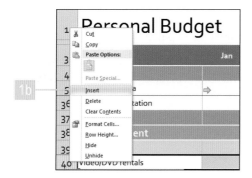

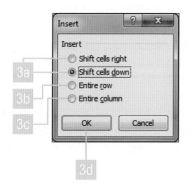

Insert rows and columns

Insert a row or column

1 To insert a row:

  a Right-click the row number below which you'd like to insert the row.

  b Click Insert.

2 To insert a column:

  a Right-click the column number to the right of where you'd like to insert the row.

  b Click Insert.

3 If prompted on how to insert a row or column:

  a Opt to shift the cells right or down.

  b Opt to input an entire row.

  c Opt to input an entire column.

  d Click OK.

Explore templates

Just as we suggested you do with Word, we'll suggest you start with a template in Excel whenever possible. Working in Excel is complicated enough without having to also worry about inputting headings, applying text formatting and creating your own formulas to perform calculations. If you want to create a personal budget worksheet, try one of the templates first. They may have everything you need and the calculations are already configured. Most of the categories will prove useful too, although you may want to add or delete budget categories and such, as applicable. If you want to create an invoice to use in your business, there are certainly enough to choose from, and they're already written, formatted and ready to use. Here's a sampling of the invoice templates. Of course, there are others – as noted in our introduction. The best way to find out what's available is to browse through them.

Explore templates

1 Connect to the Internet.

2 In Excel, click the File tab.

3 Click New.

4 Review the options under Office.com Templates.

5 Click Budgets:

   a Click any budget once to preview it.

   b Double-click it to open it.

   c Click the Back button to return to the previous screen.

6 Continue by clicking each category, exploring what's available in each.

7 Locate a template to open.

8 Double-click it to download it.

9 Note the template is now available in Excel.

10 Make changes as desired.

11 Save the file to your hard drive.

Formulas, tables, charts and databases

9

Introduction

Excel can be used to store, manage and manipulate all kinds of data, from simple things such as calculating the calories you eat each day or blood pressure averages over time, to more complex tasks such as calculating loan and mortgage amortisation or asset depreciation. You perform calculations by inputting a formula (which consists of various functions) into the appropriate cell, and then choosing the appropriate data to calculate. (For instance, you might input data into cells B3 to B15, and then in B16 calculate the total or average of those numbers.) Once you have this data and/or the desired calculations you can turn that data into charts fairly easily. You can also create tables to hold and manage your data, complete with headings you can use to sort the data, as desired.

Because creating your own calculations is not as easy as it sounds, and creating a chart or table isn't always straightforward, we suggest you look for a template that you can begin with when starting fresh. Templates already include the formulas, calculations, charts and tables you need, so you won't have to reinvent the wheel just to create, say, a profit and loss statement. However, if you can't find a template you can use or modify to suit your needs, you can certainly create and input your own formulas, or choose formulas from Excel's formula 'library' and select the cells to calculate. You can then insert your own tables and charts, although, to be truthful, we must say that using a template is far easier.

Select a range of numbers and perform a calculation

Jargon buster

Range – a range is a group or block of cells in a worksheet that have been selected or highlighted.

To manipulate multiple cells at one time you select a 'range' of cells. To select cells, you drag your mouse over them. When you've selected the cells, they may change colour. In this case, the selected cells are blue. You might select cells to create a graphic for them, such as a chart, format their contents, or cut or copy the data. In these instances it's okay to select the cells first.

When dealing with formulas, though, it's easier to first select the cell where the formula should be and its calculation will reside, and then, during formula creation, select the data to manipulate. In this instance, the selected range of cells will have a dotted line around them, denoting they are 'in limbo' and awaiting something to happen.

H	I
Total Calories	Calories to Maintain Weight, with exercise
2200	2150
2040	2150
2400	2150
2250	2150
2000	2150
2150	2150
2600	2150
2150	2150
2350	2150
2300	2150
2350	2150
2850	2150
1890	2150
2050	2150
2000	2150

For your information

Generally, you do not want to see the small blue triangle you see here in the top left corner of a cell. This often implies something is wrong with the data in the cell. However, in this instance, the formula used here simply omits the adjacent cell (which is the number of calories required to maintain one's weight), and this has sent up a red flag to Excel. However, there's nothing wrong here, and the error can be ignored.

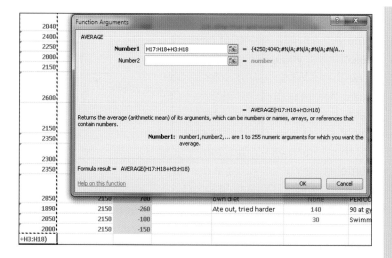

Select a range of data

1 Open a new, blank worksheet in Excel.

2 Drag your mouse over cells A1 to A10.

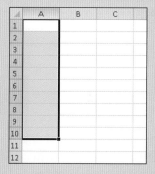

3 Now, drag from the bottom right corner from cell A10 to cell D10.

4 Press and hold the Ctrl key on the keyboard, and drag the mouse over cells G1, H1 and down to G10 and H10.

5 Click outside any selected cells to deselect all of them.

9

Did you know?

You'll see a dotted line around data you select and then opt to copy or cut, as the data is then waiting to be pasted somewhere else. The dotted line will go away once pasted.

You are not relegated to selecting contiguous data, as we've done. You can select some data by dragging your mouse over it, but then hold down the Ctrl key on the keyboard to select additional data. There are a few instances where you'd need to do this, such as if you want to exclude certain cells or include data from other areas of the worksheet.

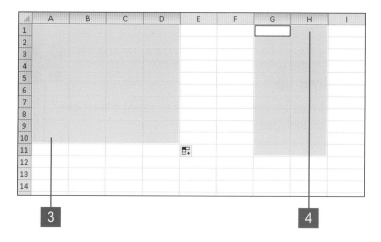

Select a range of numbers and perform a calculation (cont.)

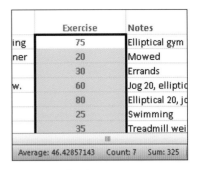

Did you know?

You can right-click a range of cells to access other options for managing or formatting the cells or cell area.

Timesaver tip

If you select a range of data that options such as sum or average can be applied to, you'll see those values in the bottom right corner of the Excel worksheet window.

Now, here's the important part. When speaking about a range of numbers you have to have some form of reference and some way of denoting the range so Excel can work with it. Say you start a range by selecting cell H3, you drag the mouse downwards, and you stop selecting cells at H18. That particular range would be defined as H3:H18. If you then add more cells and more ranges, those are separated by commas. For instance, H3:H18, H21:H28. Note that ranges don't have to occur in a single row or column. Here's an example with the selected text in blue. The range here would be fairly complex, and would start with B8:B11, B15:B19, B23:B25, F8:F11, etc.

Timesaver tip

The first step to creating a chart is to select the range of data to be included in the chart.

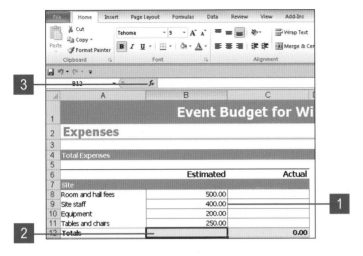

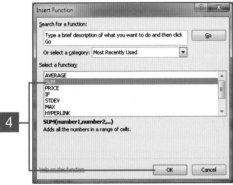

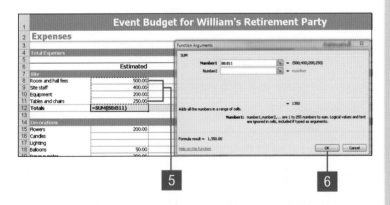

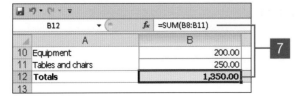

Select a range of numbers and perform a calculation (cont.)

Apply a sum

1 Input data that you'd like to add.

2 Select the cell where you'd like the sum of the range of numbers you'll select to appear. Here, we've chosen the cell next to Totals.

3 From the Home tab, click Fx.

4 In the Insert Function dialogue box, click Sum, then click OK.

5 Drag your mouse over the range of cells to add them together.

6 Click OK.

7 Notice the new formula appears next to FX and a value appears in the cell. In this case, the formula is =Sum (B8:B11) and the total is 1350.

9

Select a range of numbers and perform a calculation (cont.)

Apply an average

1. Input data that you'd like to average.
2. Select the cell where you'd like the average of the range of numbers you'll select to appear.
3. From the Home tab, click Fx.
4. In the Insert Function dialogue box, click Average, then click OK.
5. Drag your mouse over the range of cells to average.
6. Click OK.

Copy and paste a formula

1. Right-click any cell that contains a formula.
2. Click Copy.
3. Right-click the cell you want to apply the formula to.
4. Click Paste and note the options.
5. Hover the mouse over each option until you see Formulas.
6. Click it.

After you've created and applied a formula to a cell you may want to copy the formula and apply it to another range of data. While recreating formulas for simple calculations such as the sum or average isn't a big deal, recreating more complex formulas certainly is. If you've gone to the trouble of applying or creating a formula once, there's no reason to create it again.

You can copy a formula by right-clicking the cell that contains the formula and clicking Copy. Excel will copy what's in the cell, and when you're ready to paste it, you'll have the option to paste the formula, the value, the formatting or other characteristics. Depending on what you've chosen to copy, you may see options like this when pasting:

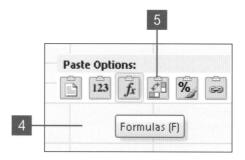

Excel has its own library of functions, and these functions are grouped into categories. You use functions to create formulas. There are a lot of available function categories, including but not limited to Financial, Math & Trig, Logical and Date & Time. There are over 50 functions in the Financial category alone, so you have lots to choose from when creating your specific formula.

Jargon buster

Function – a formula is what is inserted into a cell to denote a complete calculation; a function is a single mathematical calculation in that formula. Average and sum are functions in Excel, as is standard deviation, accrued interest and the like. You define the functions to create the formula.

You already know how to apply a formula by choosing a function. Earlier you learned how to apply the sum and average to a list of numbers. You apply other formulas similarly. You click the Fx button, you select the formula from the list, you select the data to apply it to and you click OK. So, here let's look at the basic functions you'll use most of the time.

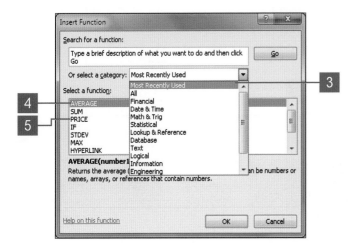

Explore basic functions

Explore basic functions

1 Click any empty cell in an Excel worksheet.

2 Click Fx.

3 In the Insert Function dialogue box, select Most Recently Used from the drop-down list.

4 Note that Average and Sum are listed first.

5 Click Price. Read the information offered.

6 Click Count. Read the information offered.

7 Continue exploring as desired.

9

Explore basic functions (cont.)

For your information

There is a multitude of help available at www.microsoft.com/excel. Click Support, click Excel and click Formulas or Function reference to get started.

Explore financial functions

1 Click any empty cell in an Excel worksheet.

2 Click Fx.

3 In the Insert Function dialogue box, select Financial.

4 Note the first option is AccrInt. That's 'accrued interest'.

5 Scroll down and select other options and read their descriptions.

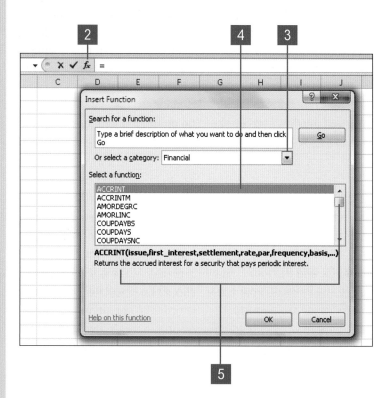

You might think, after viewing the available functions in Excel, that it's unlikely you will need a formula that can't be created with the Insert Function wizard, at least as a beginner Excel user. However, it is possible, and it happens more than you think. As an example, you may need to add a group of numbers, multiply that total by 5, and then divide the entire thing by 3.2 to obtain a result that is unique to your work, your company or even your finances. This particular formula is not available from the Insert Function dialogue box, even though its functions are (sum, product, quotient). When you find yourself in this predicament, you have to create the formula yourself. You'll need a few mathematical skills to create your own formula, which is beyond the scope of this book, but we can get you started.

You will need to keep in mind the order of operations when you create a formula; this is how numbers are calculated when there are various functions and numbers involved. The Order of Operations says that anything in parenthesis is always done first, exponents next, multiplication and division after that, and addition and subtraction last. For our example, we'd need a formula that looks something like this: =(5*(SUM(A1:A5))/3.2). You'll notice that the * means to multiply, and that the / means to divide. There are parentheses to denote in what order things should be calculated; remember parentheses are important to the order of operations because they denote what should be done first. There's also an = sign to start the equation. You see the familiar Sum function, followed by the cells to add, too.

For your information

There are other options for creating formulas, but that is beyond our scope here.

Create your own formula (cont.)

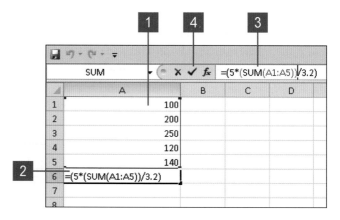

Type in a formula you've created

1 Input five numbers into five cells from A1:A5.

2 Click cell A6.

3 In the Formula Bar, type =(5*(SUM(A1:A5))/3.2)

4 Click the check mark.

?

Did you know?

You can use the Insert Function dialogue box to start a formula, and then add your own touches to it. For instance, in this example you could use the Sum function to add up all of the numbers from A1 to A5, and then in the Formula bar add the parenthesis, the *5, and the /3.2.

You create tables in Excel to organise your data, to format a group of data, or to make data easier to manage. Once you've created a table you can easily sort and filter the data in it and analyse the data independently from the other data in the worksheet. Many people create tables to simply make data 'look' prettier, which is fine too. You create basic tables from the Insert tab of Excel.

Create a basic table

For your information

When creating a table, note that you can select the cells first, and those cells can be empty or they can contain data.

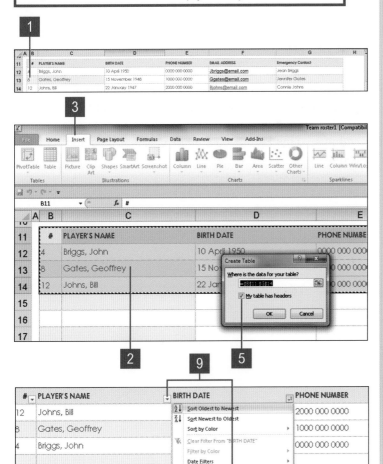

Create a basic table

1. Input some data that you can convert to a table. Include headings, such as Name, Date, Phone number, etc.

2. Select all the data you want to appear in the table, including the headers.

3. Click the Insert tab.

4. Click Table.

5. Click My table has headers.

6. Verify the range is correct, ignoring the $.

7. Click OK.

8. Click outside the new table to deselect it.

9. Note the new headings. Click the arrow by any heading to sort the data in the table by criteria you set.

Create a basic table (cont.)

Did you know?

When you sort data in a table, the data should stay intact. Here, if we sort the data by the person's age, their #, name, email address, phone number and contact information stays with it and is not lost or misplaced.

For your information

You can exclude specific data by deselecting it in the sorting options list.

Once a table has been created, you can format it in the same manner as you would in Word, PowerPoint or Outlook. You select any part of the table and click the Table Tools tab to view the options. You can easily change the colour of the table or apply style options such as banding rows (or not). You can also remove the table while keeping the data (Convert to Range). You can also hide the header row, should you decide you don't want it.

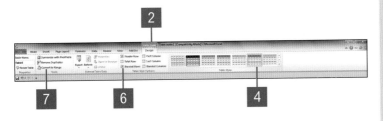

You can further format a table by selecting and then right-clicking specific cells. With a right-click you can insert or delete table rows and columns, format the cells in the table, and select the entire table, or just a row or column.

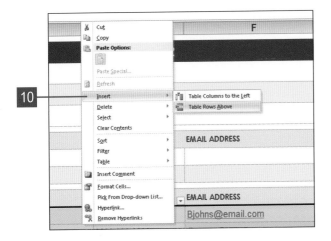

One quite useful application of table creation is to create a table that holds address book information. You can create headers for Name, Address, Phone Number, Email Address, and even headings such as Birthday or Children's Names. You can input this data manually, or if you have it in another format you may be able to import that data using the Data tab in Excel.

Format a table

Format a table

1 Click any cell in the table.

2 Click the Table Tools tab.

3 If applicable, click Design.

4 In the Table Styles group, select a new colour.

5 Deselect Header row to hide it; select it again to show it.

6 Deselect Banded Rows, and select it again to see the difference.

7 Note the option Convert to Range. This is what you'll click to remove the table, while keeping the data.

8 Select any cell or group of cells in the table.

9 Right-click it.

10 Review the options, including those to insert and delete rows and columns.

11 Click Format Cells.

12 Click OK when finished.

9

Format a table (cont.)

Create a database of names and addresses

1. Type the data required for an address book, including headings. If you like, start from a template.

2. Select the data.

3. Click the Insert tab.

4. Click Table.

5. Click My table has headers.

6. Click OK.

?

Did you know?

You can use your Contacts list in Outlook to start your new address book. You can export your contacts in Outlook as text, and then import that data from Excel's Data tab. There's a wizard in both to help you. In Outlook, click the File tab, click Open, and click Import, and then choose Export to a File (choose Tab separated values) and work through the wizard. Then, in Excel, click the Data tab and From Text, browse to the file and work through the wizard to import it.

Many of the templates you'll use with Excel will already have charts built right in. For instance, this household budget template has two charts that change as you input your own personalised data. If you can find a template that already contains a chart, we suggest you use it. Notice in this figure that the chart on top is selected, and one of the Chart Tools tabs is selected as well. You can use these Chart Tools to personalise the chart you create or 'borrow' from a template. You can even select a different chart layout or chart style, although you may have to tweak the resulting layout a bit.

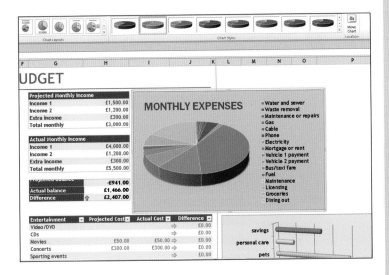

You won't always be able to find what you want in a template, though, and you'll have to input your data and create your own chart (although you can still start with a template). Here, we've input data related to cookie sales, selected the cookie type and amount sold, and then we can easily create various charts to review the data.

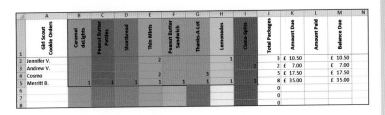

Create a basic chart (cont.)

Create a chart

1. Input and select the data to analyse in a chart.

2. Click the Insert tab.

3. In the Charts group, click the down arrow under Column, Line, Pie, Bar, Area, Scatter and Other Charts. Select one.

4. Position your mouse so that you see the four-headed arrow shown here.

5. Click and drag to move the chart.

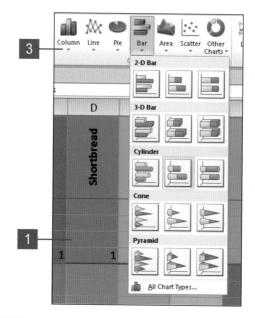

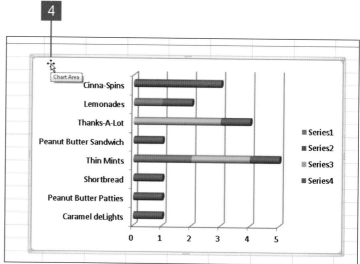

Important

If you click and drag but only move a part of the chart, stop, click the Undo button and try again. You want to select the entire chart, not just a portion of it.

Once you've created a chart, like anything else you can select it or part of it, and edit or format it. You may want to change the colour of the chart and/or choose a new chart type, as shown here. Note that you can also select various portions of the chart and delete them, such as headings, legends and the like.

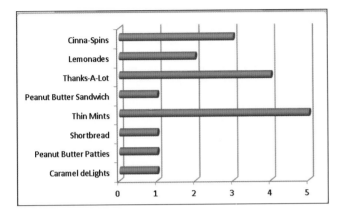

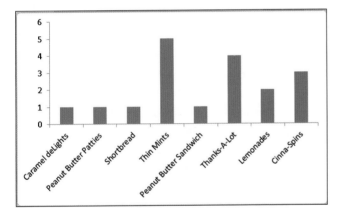

The best way to explore how to format a chart is to double-click on various parts of it. In this instance, if you double-click a bar of the chart you have the option to change how the chart looks on the page. You can change the fill, border colour, border style, and even add shadows and 3D effects, to name a few options.

Format a chart (cont.)

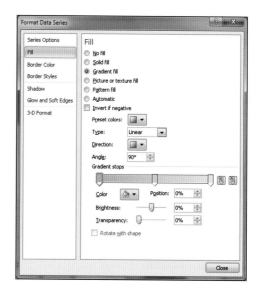

Format a chart by double-clicking

1 Select the chart you created earlier.

2 Double-click the chart itself and make changes as desired.

3 Double-click any axis and make changes as desired.

4 Right-click the text on the axis and make changes as desired.

If you double-click an X or Y axis, you'll have the option to change things about that as well. You can change the interval unit, for instance, as well as where to put the axis labels. How you apply these options depends on the chart type you've selected, so it'll be up to you to explore these options for the chart you've created.

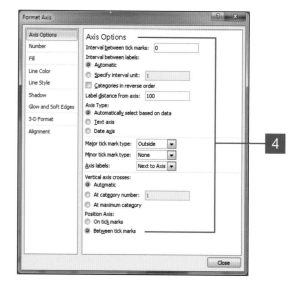

?

Did you know?

You can right-click text and choose a different font type, if desired.

You can also select a chart and format it using the Chart Tools tabs. There are three:

■ Design – to change the chart type, chart layout and chart style. You can also switch row and column data.

■ Layout – to insert items like chart title, axis labels, data labels, gridlines and more. You can also change or set a chart name.

■ Format – to format the chart with colours, outlines, fills, effects and more. You can also change the height and width of the chart.

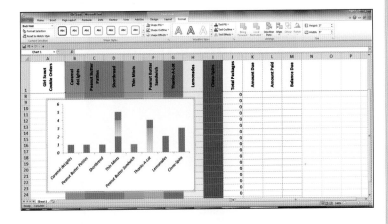

9

Format a chart (cont.)

Format a chart from the Chart Tools tabs

1 Select any chart.

2 Click the Design tab.

3 Click to explore various other chart types.

4 Click Switch Row/Column. Click again to reset.

5 Click the Layout tab.

6 Click Chart Title.

7 Click a title type.

8 Type a title name.

9 Experiment with:

a Axis Titles

b Legend

c Data Labels

10 Click the Format tab.

11 Select a new Shape Style.

12 Select a new Shape Fill.

13 Select a new Shape Outline.

14 Select a new Shape Effect.

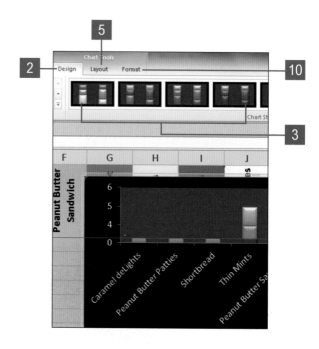

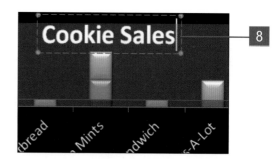

Using templates: create a budget, invoice and more

Introduction

You can now use the skills you've learned to create your own worksheets for just about any task imaginable. As you might guess, we're going to steer you towards using templates, as there's likely a template you can use as a starting point. You explored templates in Chapter 8, so in this chapter we'll focus on finding the best template for you and how you can use it to meet your needs.

Before you start this chapter, think about what you'd like to create in Excel. Perhaps you need to create a household budget to see where you can trim spending and earn more income; perhaps you've started a new business and now need a professional-looking invoice, receipt or time sheet; or maybe you want to create an inventory of everything you own for the purpose of creating an itemised will for your heirs. You can even create and print calendars for your refrigerator, complete with important meetings, birthdays, dates and events!

It's important to note that even if you don't find a template you like or that suits your needs perfectly, you'll probably get ideas for how you'd like your worksheet to look if you decide to start from scratch. You may also be able to make use of an existing template by copying some headings and formatting and pasting them into your own, blank, worksheet. You may even be able to copy a formula that's already been created, and avoid having to create the formula yourself.

What you'll do

Find the best templates

Personalise a template

Apply conditional formatting

Find the best templates

Explore Office.com

1 Connect to the Internet.

2 From your web browser, likely Internet Explorer, navigate to www.office.com

3 Scroll down to the bottom of the page and click All Templates.

You can find templates under the File menu of Excel. As you know, the templates are categorised by type, and you click a folder or icon to access the templates in the category listed. You have to be connected to the Internet to access the templates, as they are located at www.office.com and not on your computer. It's also important to remember that the available templates change often, as do their categories and subcategories. It's likely that at some point you'll open a folder only to find it's empty. However, don't let that discourage you; the templates in it may have been moved to another area, or be under a different category or name.

You can also access templates by going to www.office.com There's an entire section just for templates. You'll find more templates there than you will from the File tab – at least, that's the way it appears to us. And while browsing you may decide you'd rather use a template built for Word or PowerPoint over Excel, especially if you don't need to perform any calculations (such as is often the case with an address list or a team roster). If you don't find what you want from the File tab, try Office.com

When at Office.com, note that you can browse for templates by name. There's an option to search for templates at the top of the page. If you'd rather not browse for templates by category, as detailed below, feel free to type in a description of the template you're looking for.

Pet-sitting invoice
Excel 2003
Provided by: Microsoft

Pet-sitting invoice

6 Download

4 Select a template category.

5 Browse the available invoices. Hopefully, you'll see that using a template is better than starting from scratch!

6 If you see an invoice you like, click Download.

7 When prompted, click Save.

8 The invoice will open in Excel.

?

Did you know?

It's okay if the template is for Excel 2003, Excel 2007 or even Excel for XP; it will still work fine in Excel 2010.

10

Personalise a template

Once you have a template you can personalise it with your own data, pictures, company name and other items. You'll probably want to input some data first, and then add pictures later. If you've started a home inventory from a template, you might like to add pictures by each item you've listed. Maybe you want to add a team picture to a team roster you've previously created. In our example here, we have replaced the existing picture with one of our own, input our own data and are ready to print the invoice for the customer.

Insert a picture or clip art

1 Open any template or worksheet you'd like to personalise with a picture or clip art.

2 Click inside the worksheet near where you'd like to add the image.

3 Click the Insert tab.

4 To add a picture:

a Click Clip Art.

b Browse to the location of the file and click Insert.

c Resize the image by dragging it from the corners.

5 To add clip art:

a Click Clip Art.

b Search for and locate the clip art to add.

c Double-click it.

d Resize as necessary.

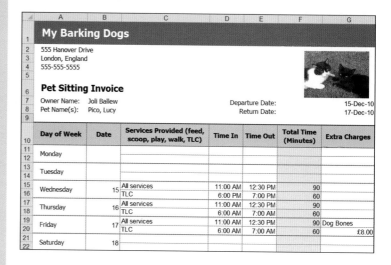

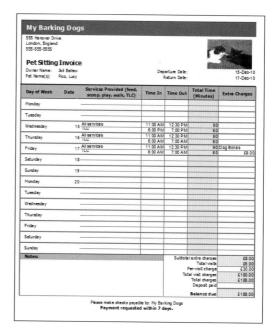

Adding pictures is just the beginning, though. You can re-format the text (perhaps changing something in italics to bold), you can replace the generic names in the template with names that suit your needs, and you can input your own data. With an invoice template, the formulas are already done for you, too. In our example, we simply type in the hours and hourly rate and the template does the rest.

Important

If there's a picture already in the template you've selected, you can select and then delete the picture before inputting your own one.

Important

Most of what is available from the Formulas and Data tabs will be greyed out while an image is selected, since you can't perform calculations on images.

Did you know?

You move any image by clicking and dragging it, and you resize it by dragging from the corners. You can also edit images by clicking them once to select them and then clicking the Picture Tools tab.

Now that you have a picture or clip art inserted, you'll want to work on the template itself. Foremost, you'll need to change the template headings. In the case of an invoice or timesheet, this may mean inputting your company's name, address and phone number. In the case of a budget, it may involve deleting or inserting budget categories. (You may not need a column named Student Loans, for instance, but may need one for Medical Expenses.) You'll have to look at the template you've selected and make changes that suit your needs.

10

Personalise a template (cont.)

Input your own headings and data

1. Select the cell that contains the data to change.

2. Type over the existing information.

3. Click outside the cell to apply.

Food (Dining Out & Groceries)	750.00	770.56	-20.56
Gasoline	400.00	384.00	16.00
Pet Supplies	50.00	36.54	13.46
Medical / Healthcare	75.00	104.23	-29.23
Personal Care	75.00	70.59	4.41
<Other Semi Variable Costs>	0.00	0.00	0.00
<Other Semi Variable Costs>	0.00	0.00	0.00
Total Semi Variable Costs	2,000.00	1,997.71	2.29
Highly Variable Costs			
Entertainment	150.00	204.89	-54.89
Gifts	50.00	42.33	7.67
Clothing	150.00	175.85	-25.85
Miscellaneous	100.00	105.00	-5.00
<Other Highly Variable Costs>	0.00	0.00	0.00
<Other Highly Variable Costs>	0.00	0.00	0.00
Total Highly Variable Costs	450.00	528.07	-78.07
Total Expenses	6,000.00	6,075.78	-75.78
Net Income	500.00	424.22	-75.78

You may have noticed that there are three tabs at the bottom of each Excel workbook you create. If you are working with a template, there may be one, two, three, or more than that. Check the bottom of the template you've selected to see if there are additional tabs. If there are multiple tabs, select them to see what's there. Note that you can rename the tabs to better represent what each tab contains. Here is a template for a 2011 calendar. Note that you can click any tab at the bottom to access that month's calendar. Once on the desired calendar, you can input your own information too. Calendars are the perfect item for your refrigerator door!

Did you know?

When you create a new, blank workbook it contains three tabs, each of which represents a worksheet. You can add or delete tabs by right-clicking on their name.

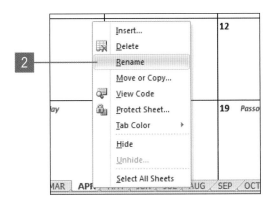

Did you know?

Right-click any tab and click Tab Color to add a colour to the tab name.

Name or rename a worksheet

1 Right-click on the tab Name.

2 Click Rename.

3 Type the new name.

Delete and hide rows and columns

1 Click the row or column title to delete or hide, such as A, B or C, or 1, 2 or 3.

2 Right-click and select Hide or Delete.

When working with a template you'll often find that you don't need all the rows and columns. Perhaps you want to delete columns for student loans, child care, or rent (when filling out a budget worksheet) or delete certain days from a timesheet because your business is not open during those hours. Perhaps you want to hide data from those who may view the worksheet, or refrain from printing certain cells while still keeping the data available when you need it, too.

For your information

To select multiple rows or columns, hold down the Shift key while selecting those that are contiguous, or the Ctrl key when selecting those that are non-contiguous.

10

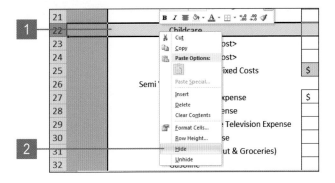

Personalise a template (cont.)

You learned in the last chapter that you can create tables to sort and filter data by size, by first or last name, by oldest to newest, by lowest to highest, and more. This helps you organise data in a specific order. Sometimes, though, you don't want to sort all the data together, you simply want to 'call out' numbers or data that has reached a certain threshold. For instance, you may want to note budgetary expenses that are more than £200/month to see if you can cut back. Or you may need to highlight workers in a timesheet as they approach 40 hours in any given week. You may need to call out a principal or interest threshold in an amortisation worksheet, or items in your home inventory that are valued above a price you set.

You can quickly scan a worksheet to find data that is above or below a specific number you set, data that contains specific text, data that is before or after a specific date, data that is in between two numbers and data that is in the top or bottom percentage in a set of data using conditional formatting.

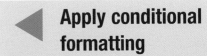

Apply conditional formatting

Apply conditional formatting

1 Select the range of data to review.

2 From the Home tab, click Conditional Formatting.

3 Click Highlight Cell Rules, then click Greater Than.

4 In the Greater Than dialogue box, type a threshold number.

5 Select a formatting colour.

6 Note the changes in the document and click OK to apply.

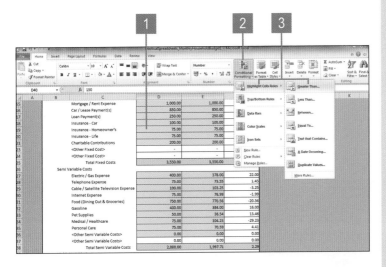

Important

Repeat these steps to apply conditional formatting for other items in the Highlight Cell Rules options and in the Top/Bottom Rules options.

10

Share and print

11

Introduction

Now that you've had some experience with Excel, you're ready to share and print the workbooks you've created. As with other Microsoft Office programs, you can save files in various formats, send files via email or upload them to a website, and you can print them when you need to physically share or put the worksheet in the post. You can review these skills in the first few chapters of this book. In this chapter we'll talk about Excel specifically, including introducing the available file types, printing single sheets or entire workbooks, and protecting your files to keep them safe.

Because Excel worksheets can, by their nature, hold sensitive data or data you do not want altered, we'll start this chapter by showing you how to turn a worksheet into a PDF file (and how to protect the file on your hard drive with a password). The PDF file format is a good option when you need to send the final version of something, such as an invoice, fund-raising budget, community centre expense report or timesheet that you do not want changed by the recipient.

What you'll do

Use PDF

Explore other file types

Protect your work

Print in Excel

!

Important

You should never send an invoice (or something equally important) to anyone in the form of a simple Excel file because the recipient could easily open the file and make changes to the totals or data.

You'll also learn how to protect a file with a password and apply other protections, such as encryption. Encryption makes it virtually impossible for someone, without the proper password, to open the file. When you protect a workbook, only you and anyone you give permission to can open the file. This allows you to keep the workbook safe from prying eyes. You can also semi-protect a worksheet or workbook by restricting what can be viewed and edited. For instance, if you've hidden certain rows or columns, you can make sure they remain hidden when the person opens it and that they cannot be un-hidden by the user.

Lastly, you'll learn how to print a workbook. While the same commands apply (File tab, Print button), there are options to print only the 'active' sheets, specific pages of a workbook and more.

To present your document to virtually anyone in the world, you can save your document as a PDF file. PDF stands for Portable Document Format and is a standard formatting option that anyone can open. Most users opt for Adobe Reader to open PDF files. There are many instances when you'd want to choose PDF over another option:

- To send completed flyers and brochures to professional printers and professional organisations so they are ready to print without additional work on the part of the recipient, loss of formatting or replacement of fonts. With a PDF, what you see is what you get. It's like a picture of your work.

- To send your Excel file to someone who does not have Excel or a way to open an Excel file, or who uses a Mac, Linux or other non-Windows-based computer. PDF files are universal, and can be opened on virtually any computer.

Did you know?

Anyone with a fairly new, Windows-based PC can download the free Excel Viewer from Microsoft. With Excel Viewer, you can open, view and print Excel workbooks, even if you don't have Excel installed. You can also copy data from Excel Viewer to another program. However, you cannot edit data, save a workbook or create a new workbook.

- To send a final invoice to a customer and to make the invoice difficult, if not impossible, to alter.

- To send a CV to a potential employer.

For your information

PDF files are not only safer and more secure than 'regular' Excel files, they also preserve formatting and fonts, so the document appears the same to the recipient as it does to you. For professional printers, this is extremely important.

Use a PDF

See also

Explore additional file types in the following sections. There are other options for saving files so that Linux and Mac users can open them, and various ways to 'protect' your work so that others can open, but not modify, the document (besides using PDF).

Use a PDF (cont.)

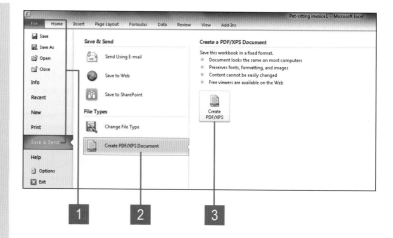

Create a PDF file

1 Click the File tab and click Save & Send.

2 Click Create PDF/XPS Document.

3 Click Create PDF/XPS.

4 If desired, change the file name.

5 Browse to the location on your computer to save the file.

6 Click Options.

7 Review the options and, for now, accept the defaults.

8 Click Publish.

9 Once saved, the new PDF file will open and you can print or email it, if desired.

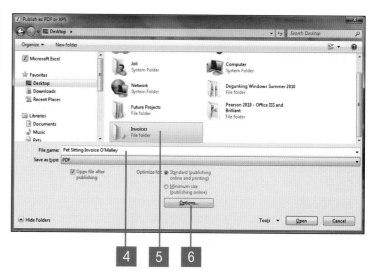

Jargon buster

XPS – the XML Paper Specification format. Similar to PDF, it retains formatting, can be read on virtually any computer and is a 'final' document ready for printing or publishing. This is how you'll send flyers, playbills, brochures and the like to a professional print shop.

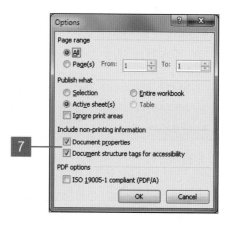

Besides PDFs, there are other file types you can opt for. You can access the additional file types in two ways. You can click File, click Save & Send, and click Change File Type, or you can click File and Save As, and access the additional file types from the Save As dialogue box. Note that by default and in both instances, Excel Workbook is selected.

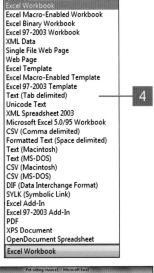

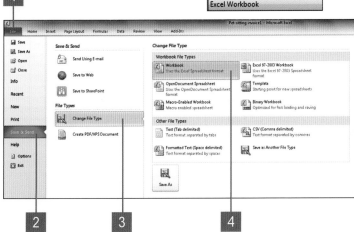

Explore other file types

1 Click the File tab.

2 Click Save & Send.

3 Click Change File Type.

4 Select the file type.

5 Name the workbook appropriately.

6 Click Save As.

The file type 'Excel Workbook' is the newest available file type and has features that earlier file type versions do not. This file type can be opened by anyone using Excel 2007 or 2010. If the recipient is using a different version, say, Excel 97 or Excel 2003, they'll have to download the 'Microsoft Office Compatibility Pack for Word, Excel and PowerPoint 2007 and later File Formats'. This enables the recipient to open, edit and save documents, workbooks and presentations in the file formats that are new in the 2007 and 2010 versions of Excel. If you'd rather not subject your family member or colleague to this task, or if you're sure they would not know how to download the Compatibility Pack, or want to, you can choose a different format specifically, the Excel 97–2003 Workbook option. This file type can be opened in earlier versions of Excel without any drama whatsoever.

Explore other file types (cont.)

You may also want to choose OpenDocument Spreadsheet. When saving in this file format, most Mac and Linux users will be able to open and edit your worksheet. OpenDocument files can be opened in OpenOffice, a suite of programs similar to the Microsoft Office suite you use. OpenOffice is a program popular with Mac and Linux users, and it's free.

There are lots of other options, as you can see. You can change the file to text or comma delimited so you can import the data into another program, for instance. You can save a workbook as a template for use with different data later. You can also save it as a PDF, which we discussed earlier.

Jargon buster

Macro – a small computer program you generate to create a shortcut for a task you perform frequently. You record a set of commands, save those commands as a macro, and then run that macro when you need to perform the same sets of commands again.

Tab delimited, Comma delimited – a text format that can be read by most computer programs. You might export your contacts in Outlook as comma delimited, and then import them in Excel using the same format.

OpenDocument – a format used in free and open source programs such as OpenOffice.org and NeoOffice. If you know you'll be sharing a file with someone who uses these programs, save it in this format first.

If you've created a legal, sensitive or a binding document in Excel, such as an expense report, inventory list or financial statement and need to share it with others, you have to make sure that the recipient can't alter the data in your document. You have to protect yourself. You also need to protect data that's stored on your computer, should your computer get hacked into. You can do this and more by applying security protection on the Excel worksheet you need to share.

Protect your work

Important

Protect your home inventories, will and power of attorney addenda, and similar legal data with a password only you and your attorney (or doctor) know. This will help keep the document safe and un-editable, should something happen to you.

Protect a workbook

1. Open the document you want to protect and click the File tab.

2. Click the Info tab.

3. Click Protect Workbook.

4. Select the desired protection.

5. Complete the process by inputting the required information. What you are prompted to input will depend on the option you selected in Step 4.

Important

If you do protect your work with passwords, make sure you write down the password and keep it somewhere safe, but away from prying eyes, identity thieves, or unscrupulous family members or co-workers.

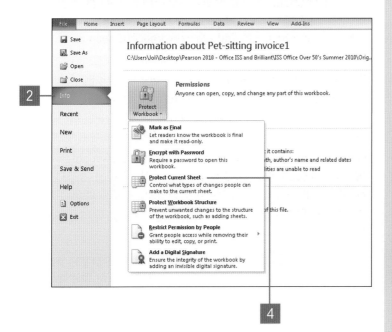

Protect your work (cont.)

You'll see six options when you opt to protect your workbook. After you make a selection, you'll be prompted accordingly. If you choose to encrypt with a password, for instance, you'll be prompted for a password. If you opt to protect the current sheet, you'll be prompted to make various decisions regarding what can and cannot be edited. Here are the options:

- Mark as final – mark a document as final and all typing, editing commands and proofing marks are disabled or turned off. The document is *read-only*. This helps prevent your recipients making changes to the document.

- Encrypt with Password – make this selection and the Encrypt Document dialogue appears. Note that if you forget the password, no one can help you. Make sure you keep the password written down and in a safe place.

- Protect Current Sheet – make this selection when you want to restrict what recipients can and cannot edit on any given worksheet.

- Protect Workbook Structure – opt for this when you want to prevent users adding or deleting worksheets or displaying hidden worksheets. You can also prevent users changing the size or position of worksheet windows. Workbook structure and window protection applies to the entire workbook.

- Restrict Permission by People – click this to restrict who can do what to a workbook. This is fairly complicated and requires an understanding of rights management, which you may not be familiar with.

- Add a Digital Signature – opt for this if you have a digital signature. Digital signatures use computer cryptography to secure data, and are provided by a third party. Like the previous option, this is complex and may not suit your needs.

Print in Excel

Print a page

1. Click the File tab, and click Print.
2. Note the Print Preview.
3. Verify Print Active Sheets is selected.
4. Click Print.

If you need to manually fax a worksheet, put it in the post or physically hand it to another person, you have to print the worksheet. As with any Office program, you'll have various print options, including Print Preview and Page Setup. Before you commit, though, use Print Preview to verify that what you're about to print is exactly what you need. You can access the Print Preview and Page Setup options from the File tab, in Print.

Here are some tips for using Print Preview:

■ If there are multiple pages, click to preview each page.

■ If the print out isn't going to look the way you want it to, switch from Portrait Orientation to Landscape Orientation or select a new paper size.

■ Select Print Entire Workbook instead of Print Active Sheets.

To print fewer pages, hide blank rows and columns.

If you are unable to get the perfect fit for your data using the Print Preview techniques just introduced, you may be able to make improvements using Page Setup. You may want to scale the worksheet to fit, change the margin size, add headers and footers, or define the print area.

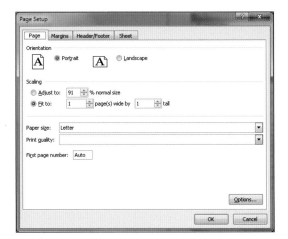

Print a workbook

1. Click the File tab, and click Print.

2. Note the Print Preview.

3. Verify Print Entire Workbook is selected.

4. Click Print.

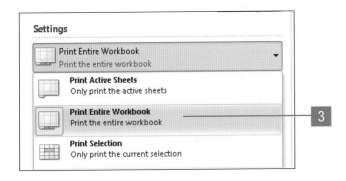

Print in Excel
(cont.)

Outlook and email

Introduction

Microsoft Outlook is the email management program included with various editions of Microsoft Office 2010. You may choose to use Outlook to send and receive email only, but note that you can also maintain a calendar, manage your contacts and keep notes and create tasks. If you decide not to use all of these features, that's okay; if you already keep a written calendar and to-do list and don't want to change, you don't have to. You will want to learn how to manage emails that you want to keep, though, as well as how to send interesting emails complete with pictures and formatting to your children and grandchildren. You'll need to manage your junk email too; there's simply no way around it – you'll get spam. No matter how you ultimately decide to use Outlook, there's a lot to learn and explore.

To use Outlook effectively, you need to first input your email address information, understand the Outlook interface and know what Outlook offers. That's what you'll learn first. In this chapter you'll learn the basics, including inputting email account information, reading and responding to email, formatting email and inserting pictures and similar 'introductory' tasks. In later chapters you'll learn about other features, such as the Calendar and Contacts, and how to manage the mail you want to keep long-term.

What you'll do

Set up Outlook and expore the interface

Email basics

Compose an email

Change settings and explore views

Set up Outlook and explore the interface

You may currently get your mail from a web page on the Internet or with an email program like Outlook Express, Mail or Windows Live Mail. You may also use an older version of Outlook. No matter what you use, when you start Outlook for the first time you'll be asked to set it up and input information regarding your email account(s). If you've already set up Outlook or if someone has set it up for you, skip ahead to the next section.

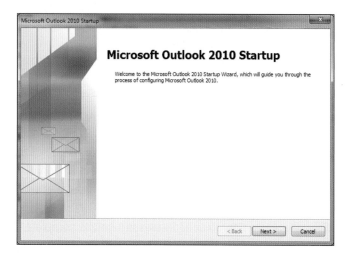

During the set-up process, you'll be prompted first for your display name, email address and password. Your display name is the name you'd like people to see when they receive email from you. It can be anything you want, but generally, people use their first and last name. Your email address and password were assigned to you by the entity that gave you your email address. Your email is the thing with the @ sign (mine is Joli_ Ballew@hotmail.com, and I love getting email from readers). You may have been given your email address by your Internet service provider, or it may be an address you obtained from Hotmail, Windows Live, Yahoo!, AOL, MSN or another entity.

Much of the time, Outlook is capable of setting up your email address with only this information. When that happens, all is right with the world! When Outlook cannot set up your email account automatically, though, you will have to input the information manually. To get this information you'll have to search for the settings on the Internet or call or contact your email provider. We suggest you get someone on the phone and have them walk you through it, should this happen.

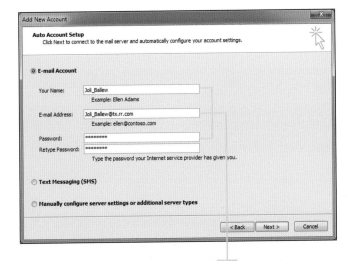

Set up an email account

1 Open Microsoft Outlook.

2 When prompted to create an email account, verify Yes is selected and click Next.

3 If you are prompted to upgrade account settings from another email program, follow the prompts to do that.

4 If prompted regarding the type of account to create, choose email account and click Next.

5 Input the required information, including your display name (this can be anything), your email address and your password.

12

Set up Outlook and explore the interface (cont.)

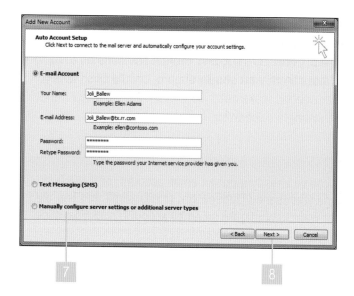

6 Wait to see if Outlook can configure the email account on its own. If it cannot, opt to set up your connection without encryption. (You'll be prompted.)

7 If this doesn't work, select Manually configure server settings or additional server types.

8 If you have to manually configure settings, call your ISP for the information to input. Input the information, then click Next.

9 Click Close and Finish when the information has been successfully entered.

10 Review the email in your Inbox.

Important

You must be connected to the Internet to retrieve your email.

For your information

If you have problems setting up your email, remember that passwords are case-sensitive. Also, note that you may have to call your Internet service provider to help you input the proper settings.

To understand Outlook, you have to be comfortable with the interface and be able to navigate through it. Although it looks quite complex initially, it only takes a few minutes to decipher it. In fact, the Ribbon should already look familiar, and you can, of course, make out the calendar. Spend a few minutes now locating the following items:

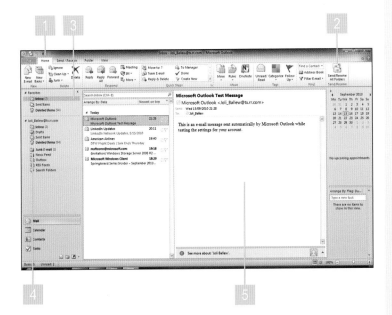

Tabs – Outlook has five tabs: File, Home, Send/Receive, Folder and View. The Home tab is where you'll spend most of your time.

Send/Receive button – here you can manually check for email (Outlook checks every 30 minutes by default). Just click the Send/Receive button.

Inbox – this is one of several 'folders' in the Navigation pane. To access new email, make sure Inbox is selected. Other folders include Sent Items, Deleted Items, Junk E-Mail and others.

Navigation pane – the pane that holds the folders and offers access to other areas of Outlook, including the Calendar and Contacts. If Outlook looks funny to you, make sure Mail is selected at the bottom of this pane.

Reading pane – this is the pane where you can read any selected email. You can move this so that it appears under your list of emails from the View tab.

Email basics (cont.)

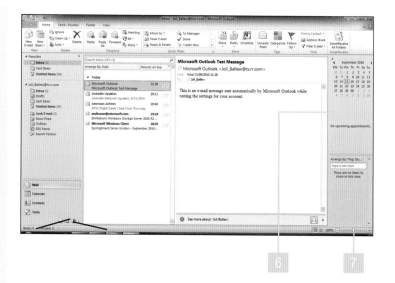

6   To-do Bar – this pane on the far right offers access to a calendar, appointments and tasks. You can minimise or remove this pane from the View tab.

7   Status bar – to review progress of the current task or its current status. Here you can see there are five items and two are unread.

8   Zoom slider – available from the Status bar; you can move the zoom slider to zoom in and out of emails in your Inbox.

Receive and read email

1   In Outlook, click the Home tab.

2   Verify Inbox is selected in the left pane.

3   Click Send/Receive All Folders.

4   Select any email in the Inbox.

5   Read the contents of the email in the Reading pane.

6   To delete any email, from the Home tab, click Delete.

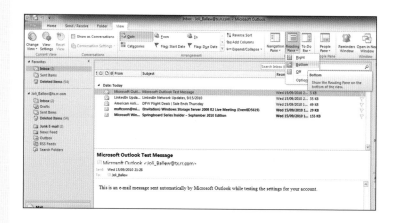

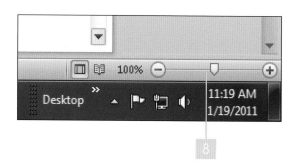

If you do not have any emails in your Inbox, you can always write one *from* yourself *to* yourself. You can email me at joli_ballew@hotmail.com and I'll send a reply too (just tell me that you are reading my book!).

You may come across an email you'd like to reply to or send to someone else to share it. You may want to forward email that contains a funny joke, pictures of the grandchildren, or an invitation to a retirement party or reunion, for instance. You may simply want to reply to an email. In most instances, people will expect a response of some sort, but they do not like to receive emails that don't say anything or have any substance either. If the email warrants a response, try to reply quickly.

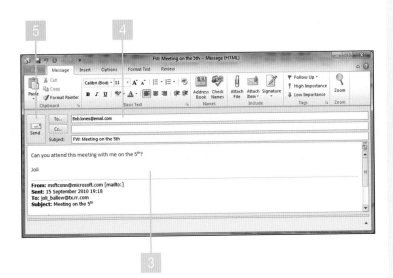

Reply to and forward email

1 Select any email to respond to or forward.

2 From the Home tab, click Reply, Reply All or Forward.

3 Write your response in the body of the email.

4 If applicable, type an email address in the To: line or the CC or BCC lines.

5 Click Send.

Did you know?

When you forward an email, all parts of the email are sent, including attachments and pictures.

Email basics (cont.)

Jargon buster

Reply – to reply to the sender of the email only, if other email addresses are included in the CC line.

Reply All – to reply to everyone who received the email from the sender. If there are people in the CC line, they'll get your response. (You won't know if people are in the the BCC line and no response to them would be sent.)

CC – Carbon Copy. People put email addresses here for recipients who should read the email but do not necessarily need to respond to it.

BCC – Blind Carbon Copy. People put email addresses here for people who need to see and read the email without letting others know they are included in the recipient list.

There are times when you'll need to print an email. You may need to print dates and times for an event or a map with turn-by-turn directions. You may want to print a flyer to share it with a group or club. Who knows, you may even get some digital artwork from a grandchild you'd like to put on the refrigerator door!

Just as you do with other Microsoft programs, you'll click the File tab to get to the Print command. You can select a printer, choose a style and preview the email you want to print to see how it'll look on paper. If you like what you see, click Print. If you don't like what you see, click Print Options. There you can select the number of copies as well as which pages to print, if applicable. Here the email is 10 pages, however, we've opted to only print page 1 and page 2.

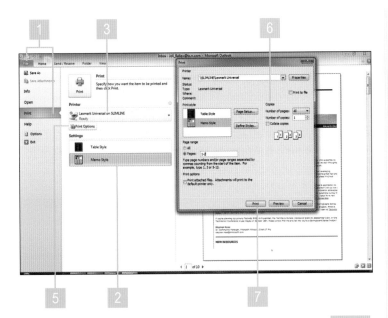

Print an email

1. In Outlook, click the File tab, and click Print.

2. Click Memo Style.

3. Verify the printer you want to use is selected.

4. If you need to zoom in on the preview, click it once. (Click again to zoom back out.)

5. Click Print Options.

6. Configure the options as desired.

7. Click Print, Preview or Cancel.

Did you know?

You can print from any folder, including Sent, Deleted and even Junk E-Mail.

For your information

If the Print Preview shows that the entire first page of an email you want to print contains the email addresses of other recipients, or that the last page is just a signature or picture, in Print Options, specify only the pages you want to print (and thus, those you do not) prior to printing.

People often attach files to emails. These files can be anything from a sales brochure to a budget spreadsheet; from a slide presentation to a video montage. You'll more likely receive pictures and videos, though, as people send a lot of this type of media via email.

You can preview many types of attachments inside the Reading pane of Outlook. Here is an email message with an attachment titled DSCN0505 (2).jpg. It's a picture. Note

Email basics (cont.)

Open, view and save attachments

1 Select the email that contains the attachment.

2 To view the attachment:

a If the attachment can be previewed, click it once. You'll see it in the Reading pane.

b If the attachment can't be previewed and you're sure it's safe, double-click the attachment. You'll see it in its related program.

3 To save an attachment:

a While previewing in Outlook, from the Attachment Tools tab, click Save As.

b While previewing in another program, click File and Save As (or something similar).

c In the Save As dialogue box, browse to the location to save the file and click Save.

4 To save the email and attachment in Outlook:

a Leave the email in the Inbox.

b Drag the email to any folder you've created in the Navigation page. (Refer to Chapter 14 for help creating a folder.)

that the information here shows there's a message, which is selected, and the picture attachment, which is not. If you select the picture you can preview it. (To exit this preview mode and return to the message, click Message.) You can also preview Excel files, Word documents and more. To find out if the attachment can be previewed, click it once. Note also that you can right-click any attachment and click Save As to save it to your computer's hard drive, or double-click the attachment to open it in a compatible program.

While many attachments are safe to preview and open, many are not. Attachments are the cause of almost all of the viruses you'll get via email and Outlook, so you have to be careful. Always make sure you know who the attachment is from, what it likely is, and that the sender sent it to you because they wanted to (and not because their computer was infected and the message was sent automatically). If you're in doubt, email the sender, ask them what the attachment contains and verify they sent it before you open it. The same holds true for clicking links inside an email; if you aren't sure, don't click it.

If after previewing or opening an attachment you decide you want to save it, you have lots of options, one of which you've already briefly explored (Save As). Here are some others:

▓ You can save the email that contains the attachment in your Inbox or a folder you'll create.

▓ You can open the attachment in its native program by double-clicking it (videos in Media Player and Word documents in Word, for instance), and opt to save from inside the program.

▓ You can right-click the attachment, choose Save As and save the data to your hard drive.

▓ You can click the attachment, then from the Attachment Tools tab that appears, choose Save As.

For your information

If you want to see the BCC line in Outlook, in a new message click the Options tab and then click BCC.

Compose an email

When you compose your own email you can add text and formatting, pictures and even tables, shapes and text boxes. You can add a background colour, a theme and even use tools like Cut, Copy, Paste and Format Painter. Much of this should already be familiar if you've worked through previous sections in this book, so we won't go into too much detail here. Suffice to say that if you can insert a picture in Word, PowerPoint or Excel, you can also insert a picture in an email message in Outlook. Likewise, if you can create a table in any other Office program, you can insert a table in to an email too.

Compose a new message

1 In Outlook, in the Mail view, click New E-Mail from the Home tab.

2 Type the email address of the desired recipient in the To line.

3 Type a subject.

4 Type a message.

5 From the Message tab, apply the formatting options you desire.

6 From the Insert tab, click Picture to add a picture.

7 Click Send.

See also

Chapter 2, Explore Common Features, to learn how to format text, insert and edit a picture, insert a table and more.

See also

Chapter 3, Use Find and Replace; Use the Format Painter; Select and Replace Text.

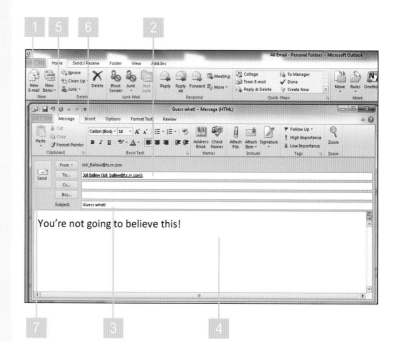

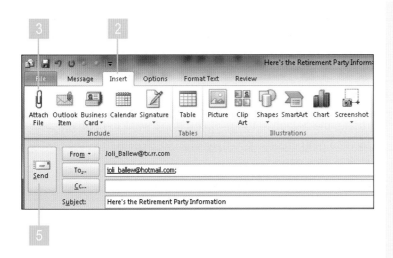

Attach a File

1. Compose a new message, or reply to or forward an existing message.

2. Click the Insert tab.

3. Click Attach File.

4. Browse to the location of the file and double-click it.

5. Complete the email message and click Send.

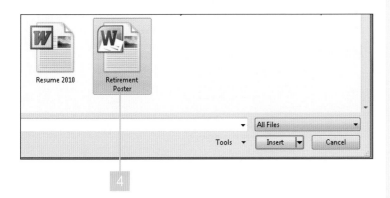

12

Change settings and explore views

All Microsoft Office programs offer a way to configure settings to personalise the program and an option for changing views. Although there are literally hundreds of changes you have the option to make, there are a few that stand out. For instance, if you have an always-on Internet connection, you may want Outlook to check for mail more often than every 30 minutes (that's the default setting). If you don't want to be distracted by incoming emails, you may want to change that to a much longer time period.

Change how often Outlook checks for email

1 In Outlook, click File.

2 Click Options.

3 Click Advanced and scroll to access Send/Receive (if necessary).

4 Click Send/Receive and change how often to check for new mail. Here it's set to 5 minutes.

5 Click Close.

6 Click OK.

You'll also want to configure your junk email options, to keep as much spam out of your Inbox as possible. Outlook has a built-in junk email filter and it's already configured, and the current settings in the filter may be working just fine for you. However, if you're still getting a lot of spam, you can raise the bar, so to speak. You can up the protection.

If you do opt to increase the junk email filter, it's important to understand that some legitimate email will be flagged as junk and sent to the Junk E-Mail folder (in the Navigation pane). Outlook guesses at what is spam and what isn't, and it will guess wrong on occasion. When this happens, though, you can tell Outlook that an email in the folder is not junk. All you have to do is right-click the email, choose Junk, and choose Not Junk. When you do this, the same sender will not be flagged again. You'll notice other options too, including to never block the sender or the sender's domain.

Did you know?

'Chatting' is quicker than sending email and is better for short online conversations. Ask your children and grandchildren what messaging program they use and get it. Then you can converse with them more easily when you're online. (We prefer the free Windows Live Messenger, from Microsoft's Windows Live suite.)

12

Change settings and explore views (cont.)

Explore Junk E-mail Options

1. From the Home tab, click Junk.

2. Click Junk E-Mail Options.

3. Read the options. For more protection, click High.

4. Click OK.

5. In the Navigation pane, click the Junk E-Mail folder.

6. Review any email in it.

7. If you find legitimate email in the Junk E-Mail folder:

   a Right-click it.

   b Click Junk.

   c Click Not Junk.

   d Review the options. Select the first option to trust email, but do not select the second.

   e Click OK.

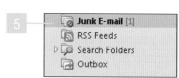

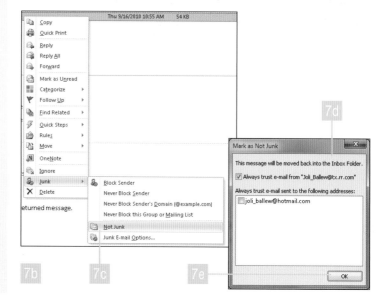

Finally, there are various ways to view things in Outlook. In general, you can switch between various views including Mail, Contacts, Calendar, Notes, Tasks and other views. You switch between views using the icons at the bottom of the Navigation pane. Those options can be configured to take up more or less space on the Navigation pane by dragging from the top of the section. Here are three views of the same area of the Navigation pane (the bottom). Note that in each instance Mail is selected. If you select a different option, the entire view of Outlook will change to reflect that choice.

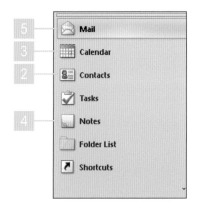

Thus, when in Mail view you see everything related to email. You have access to all of your email folders, accounts, your Inbox and the familiar options on the Home, Insert, Folder and View tabs. If you click, say, Calendar, all of that changes. (You return to the Mail view by clicking Mail in the Navigation pane.)

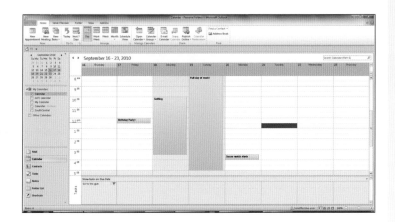

Explore Views

1. In Outlook, locate the navigation options at the bottom of the Navigation pane. You may see names and icons, only icons, or a combination of both.

2. Click Contacts.

3. Click Calendar.

4. Click Notes.

5. Click Mail.

12

See also

Chapter 13, Contacts, Calendar, Notes and Tasks.

Contacts, Calendar, Notes and Tasks

Introduction

Outlook offers much more than a way to manage your email. It comes with a calendar, an address book, and the option to create and manage tasks and notes. If you take the time to enter calendar events, create detailed contacts and use Outlook to list and manage tasks, you'll be better organised and have easy access to the information you need. Before we get started, let's look briefly at the Calendar, Contacts, Notes and Tasks.

The Calendar feature is a fully fledged calendar. It works as you'd expect; you can input important dates, set reminders and even create recurring events. Calendar entries appear in the To-do pane, too, so you'll never be in the dark about what you have in your schedule for the day. Here, the top entry is a Calendar event; the bottom entry is a Task.

The Contacts feature enables you to easily add, edit and manage the people you, well, contact. It's more than a repository for email addresses, though; a Contact Card can hold a picture, phone number, street address, birthday, anniversary, and even a website address or a map to the contact's home or business. Here's a Contact Card. Notice in the Navigation pane that there are various Contact groups. What you see in this list will differ from what's shown here.

Tasks and Notes are two more features of Outlook. Tasks are somewhat like chores; they are things that need to be done and can, perhaps, be assigned or delegated to another person. Notes are designed to be reminders to yourself. If you use yellow sticky notes, you're going to love Notes.

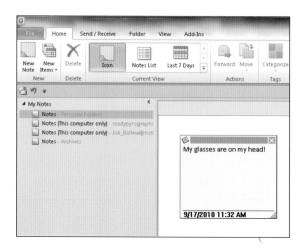

Beyond the actual features, it's important to know that you can share all of this with others by including it in an email; you can invite people to attend an event or join you for an appointment, attach a contact card and create and share (or delegate) tasks. You can even email a note!

See also

As noted in Chapter 12, you learned how to change the views in Outlook at the bottom of the left pane. The default view is Mail view, but there's also an icon for Calendar, Contacts, Tasks and Notes. You switch views by clicking the appropriate icon at the bottom of the Navigation pane.

13

Contacts ▶

Your Contact list contains all of the people you've already added as contacts. These contacts may have been acquired from a previous email program, from contacts you keep in a Hotmail account, or even contacts from an instant messaging program. Of course, you could have added them manually too. You can browse contacts to review information about them, edit the information, or share it. You can think of the Contacts feature in Outlook as a Rolodex on steroids!

You can use the Contacts feature to do more than manage your contacts, though. You can use it to your advantage in a number of other ways. For instance, if you have trouble remembering information about a person, such as a spouse's name or a friend's children's names, what day of the week the man is coming to mow your lawn, a friend's pet's name, or even a friend's street address, you can add it here and refer to it as necessary.

You can view your contacts in many ways:

- While in Contacts view, you can click any contact card to view it.

- While in Mail view, from the Home tab, click Address Book.

- While composing a new email, click the To: button (or Address Book).

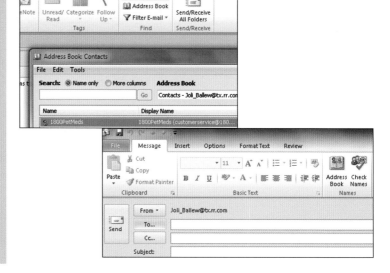

Important

When creating contacts, add as much information as possible, including phone numbers, addresses and other data. That data can be synced to devices capable of being synced with Outlook, such as the iPad, iPhone, BlackBerry and others.

You should try to actively add contacts and related information for all of the people you communicate with. Even if you don't have an email address, you can add a telephone number, website, or fax number and create a digital Rolodex for yourself. Of course, you should make sure to add contact information for everyone you email; that's a given.

A simple way to add a contact is to right-click the sender's name in an email you've received (from the Reading pane). When you do this, a Contact Card is created and you are offered the option of accepting the information that's already input or editing it. If you don't have an email handy, though, you can start a Contact Card from scratch.

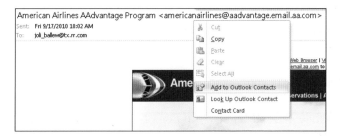

13

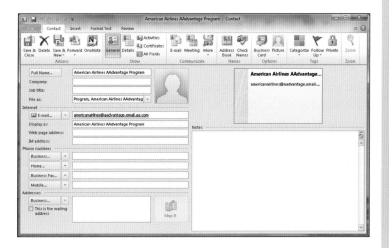

Contacts (cont.)

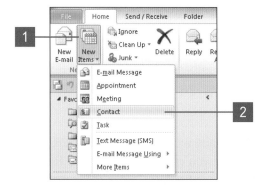

Add a contact

1 In any view, from the Home tab, click New Items.

2 Click Contact.

3 Fill in as much as you like from the Contact tab.

4 Explore the other tabs, inputting information as desired.

5 When finished, click Save & Close.

Add a contact from an email

1 In your Inbox, select an email.

2 Right-click the contact name or the email address on the email in the Reading pane.

3 Click Add to Outlook Contacts.

4 Type the desired information about the contact in all tabs.

5 Click Save & Close.

Did you know?

To insert a picture for a contact, click the picture place holder on the Contact tab and browse to the picture to use.

Did you know?

If the contact has already been added, you'll be prompted to edit or change the information.

You will need to edit a contact's information if they get a new email address, move, or perhaps even if they get a new telephone number, depending on how much information you keep about a person and how you use your contact lists. You may also want to edit a contact to add a picture you've recently acquired, too. What's nice about adding pictures is that when you get an email from a person and you have a picture in the Contact Card, you'll see the picture at the bottom of the Reading Pane. Also, if you sync Outlook with a mobile device, generally, the picture will sync too.

!	☆	🗋	🖉	From	Subject	Received ▲	Size	Categories	▽
▲ Date: Today									
	🗋			Joli Ballew	Testing to view picture	Fri 9/17/2010 11:56 AM	26 KB		

Testing to view picture
Joli Ballew <Joli_Ballew@txrr.com>
Sent: Fri 9/17/2010 11:56 AM
To: Joli Ballew

For your information

If you add a picture to your own contact card, as I've done here, it won't travel with your outgoing email. The pictures you add to your own contacts in your Address Book are there for your use only, and those pictures are not attached to any outgoing email. Thus, if your recipients want to have a picture of you appear on their own computer when they receive an email from you, they'll have to add your picture to their contacts themselves.

When you have a group of people you communicate with often, you know how time consuming it is to type all of their email addresses in the To: line or select them all from the Address Book. There's a better way. You can create a group and put their email addresses in it, and then, the next time you want to send an email to all of them, just type the group name in the To: line.

Consider creating a contact group for members of any group to which you belong or manage. For instance, if you're producing a theatre production, create a group that contains all of your cast members and stage hands. If you are managing a football club, create a group that contains all of its members. If you're part of a quilting group, rowing club or golf league, do the same. With a group created you can easily send an email to everyone in it without having to input each of their addresses in the To: line manually. You only need to type the group's name.

View and edit contacts

1. To edit a contact, use any method detailed earlier to locate the contact.

2. Double-click the contact to open the Contact window.

3. Edit as desired, and when finished, from the Contacts tab, click Save & Close.

13

Contacts (cont.)

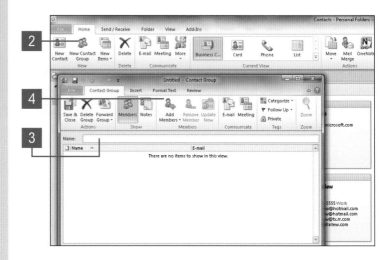

Create a contact group

1. Click the Contacts icon in the Navigation pane to open Contacts view.

2. In Contacts view, from the Home tab, click New Contact Group.

3. In the Contact Group window, type a name for the group.

4. Click Add Members.

5. When prompted to choose from where to obtain the contacts, choose Outlook Contacts.

6. Work through the list, double-clicking members to add. Click OK when finished.

7. With contacts added, click Save & Close.

Important

If you don't find the contacts you're looking for in Outlook Contacts, try another option, like Address Book.

Did you know?

If when sending an email to the group you do not want to divulge every member's email address and contact name to everyone else, put the group name in the Bcc line of a new email. Put your own email address in the To: line.

At some point you may be asked to share contact information with another person. You can either reply to them with the person's email address or attach the contact card you have on file for them. Before you send a contact card, though, make sure that what you've input in the card doesn't divulge more information than the person would be comfortable with. For instance, if the contact card has their home address, they may not want that information shared. (To be safe, we suppose it would be better not to send any contact information at all, but instead forward the request to the person who is trying to be contacted.) If you do decide to send a contact card, click Reply, click Insert, click Outlook Items, click Contacts and locate the card to attach.

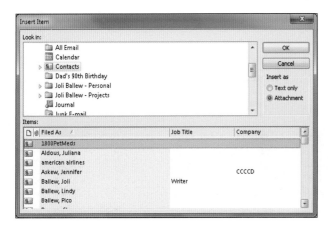

Calendar

At the bottom of the left pane, you'll see an icon that looks like a calendar. It will be in one of the forms detailed at the end of Chapter 12, so you may see it in a list or as a simple icon. Either way, click the Calendar option to get to Calendar view. (You have to click the Mail icon to return to Mail view.)

When you first enter Calendar view, you may see more than one calendar. Some people use an online calendar from Google, sync a calendar they keep on their iPhone or BlackBerry, or use a calendar from Live.com. If you've used calendars before you may have subscribed to others' calendars. If that's the case, you'll see more than one calendar, as shown here. If this is your first time using any kind of digital calendar, you'll only see one calendar.

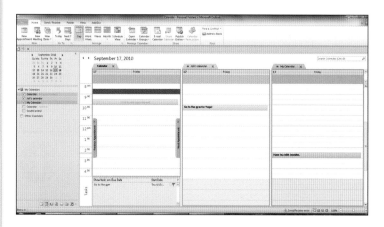

For your information

When you use Outlook's Calendar feature to store and manage your day-to-day activities, events, appointments and the like, each day when you open Outlook you can easily see (in the To-do bar) what's in store for that day. This will allow you to focus on more important things, like your grandchildren or your tennis game!

If you have multiple calendars, deselect every one of them except Calendar. 'Calendar' is the default calendar that comes with Outlook, and that's the one we'll focus on here. Note that at the top of the Home page you have the option to change the view of any calendar: Day, Work Week, Week and Month. Click these to explore the views.

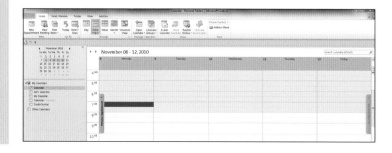

To fully utilise the calendar you have to add appointments or events. You can also add birthdays, sports tournaments or even a list of what you want to accomplish on a specific day. You input appointments and events by double-clicking any date (and/or time) on the calendar. When you do that, a new window opens: the Appointment window. You'll notice in that window that the Insert, Format Text and Review tabs offer options related to the appointments you create. Use the tabs to include or attach pertinent information, such as your travel itinerary or e-tickets, your latest lab results or a spreadsheet that contains this week's football pool.

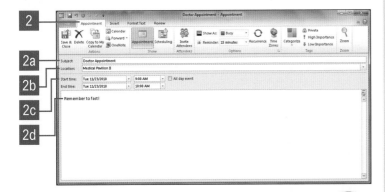

For your information

If you click All day event, the Appointment tab changes to an Event tab and the start and end times become unavailable. Outlook considers this an all-day commitment.

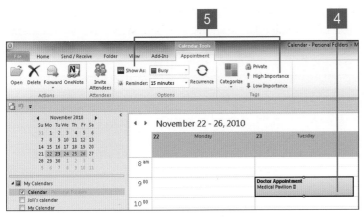

Add an appointment

1. Double-click any time or date in any calendar.

2. From the Appointment tab, input the appropriate information:

   a A subject in the Subject line.

   b A location in the Location line.

   c The start and end times. (Notice the arrows.)

   d Notes regarding the appointment.

3. From the Appointment or Event tab, click Save & Close.

4. Click the new appointment or event in the calendar.

5. Note the new Calendar Tools tab and the options on it.

13

Did you know?

You can double-click any appointment to edit it. (Just remember to click Save & Close when you've finished editing.)

Calendar (cont.)

As you can see from both the Appointment window and the Calendar Tools tab, you can configure Outlook to remind you with a sound and pop-up box before an appointment or event. Consider entering events for birthdays and anniversaries, and then set a reminder for a few days prior. The option to create a reminder is available during appointment creation. And, if the event is a birthday or anniversary, configure the event to recur. (Just click Recurrence.) Configure a yearly recurrence for birthdays, anniversaries, yearly golf tournaments and family reunions; configure weekly recurrences for exercise classes or visits with the kids.

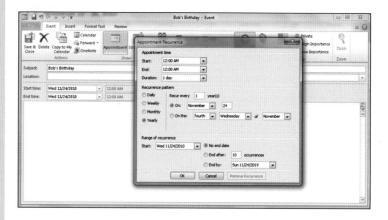

Finally, sometimes you need to let someone know about an event and ask them to attend, for instance, an all-day golf tournament, a sailing excursion or a weekend away. You may also want to ask someone to attend an appointment, too, perhaps one you have with a doctor or a lawyer. When you invite someone using Outlook, you can also request a response.

Important

!

For the recipient to be able to properly view and respond to a request, they also need to be using Outlook.

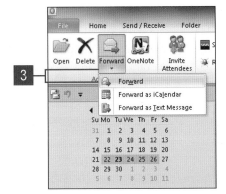

Important

If you send the appointment or event in iCalendar format, the recipient must have a compatible program on their computer to open it. Other Outlook users and those that incorporate Google Calendar will be capable, but it's important to note that many others won't have compatible programs. When in doubt, simply forward the event.

Email a Calendar event or appointment

1 In any calendar view, locate the appointment to share.

2 Click to select the appointment and to view the Calendar Tools tab.

3 Click the arrow under Forward and click Forward again.

4 Complete the email and send it.

13

We know that your children and granchildren don't really think you're that busy! If you ever need to share with them a week from your calendar to prove you actually do stuff, you can. You may want to share a week from your calendar to lay out your schedule for your boss as well. Although there are several ways to send a part of your calendar, attaching it to a new email is easiest.

Calendar (cont.)

Email a week from your calendar

1 Click the Mail icon to access the Mail view.

2 Click inside the body of the email and click the Insert tab.

3 Click Calendar.

4 Configure the options as desired. Make sure you select the proper calendar and time frame, and configure additional options as desired.

5 Click OK.

6 Complete the email and click Send.

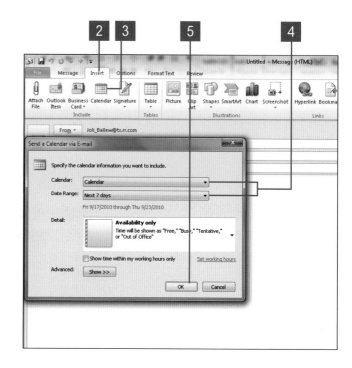

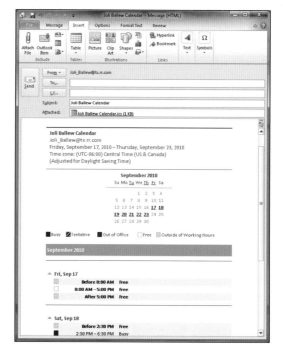

There's really not much we can say about Notes except to say you use them just as you'd use regular Post-it® notes. Notes you create look and behave like the sticky notes you're used to and are just as easy to use. Notes remain in the Notes view until you manually delete them and you can drag them from there to the Desktop or place the notes 'on top of' other programs. Here's proof.

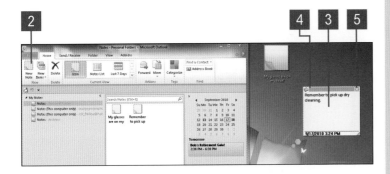

Create a note

1. Click the Notes icon in the Navigation pane.

2. Click New Note.

3. Type your note.

4. Click the top of the note, hold down the left mouse key and drag the note to the desired position on the screen.

5. Click the 'X' in the top right corner of the note to delete it. This removes the note from the screen but not from Notes view.

6. Right-click the note in Notes view to delete it or forward it.

13

You can manage notes by right-clicking them or by simply clicking the 'X' in the top right corner to delete them. In Notes view you can also change the view, forward the note in an email and even change the colour of the note.

Notes (cont.)

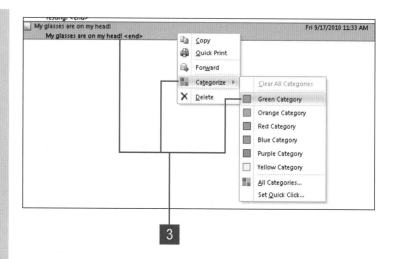

Manage notes

1 Enter Notes view.

2 Click Icon, then click Notes List.

3 Right-click any note, click Categorize and select a new colour.

4 Select any note and from the Home tab, click the 'X' to delete.

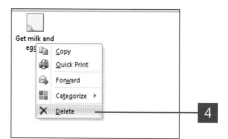

Tasks are things you have to do. Perhaps you have to deliver a contract to a colleague, pick up groceries from the local supermarket, mow the lawn, wash the dog, make a phone call to the utility company or something similar. Tasks aren't items you'd put on a calendar, necessarily, although you could, but tasks aren't simple notes either.

You create and edit a task in virtually the same way you create and edit an appointment. The window even looks the same. And you can manage tasks in in a similar manner as well. You can view tasks in different ways and edit them by double-clicking, too. When creating a task note a task title may be all you need, or you may want to fill out various information about the task, perhaps even attaching files and data to it. You can even delegate the task to another person!

You can create a new task in a number of ways, but for now let's focus on opening the Task window to create your task:

■ In any view, from the Home tab, click New Items and click Task. This will open a Task window where you can input information related to the task.

■ In Tasks view (click the Task icon at the bottom of the Navigation pane), from the Home tab, click New Task.

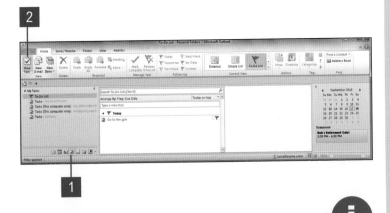

Tasks

Add and edit a task

1 Enter Task view.

2 From the Home tab, click new Task.

13

For your information

If you just want to create a task that consists only of a task title, click the 'Type a new task' window.

Tasks (cont.)

Once you've opened a new task, you simply fill out the required information, just as you did with an appointment. As usual, explore the various tabs and note that you can personalise the tasks in many ways.

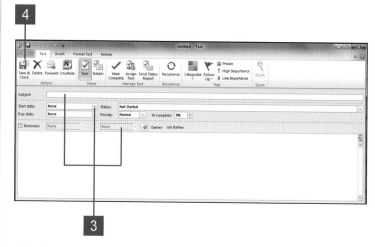

After inputting task information you can:

- Click Forward to forward the task to someone else to share it.
- Click inside the body of the task to activate the Zoom option. If you have trouble reading the task, use Zoom to increase the size.
- Assign the task to someone else.
- Input the progress to completion of the task.
- Mark the task complete.
- Attach an item to the task, such as an itinerary, map or security code.

3 Enter the task information.

4 Click Save & Close.

5 To edit the task, double-click it.

6 Add any notes about the task in the body of the Task window.

7 Check the Reminder box to create a reminder.

8 Use the drop-down lists to apply a status, priority or set a percentage of completion.

9 Note the option to mark Complete on the Ribbon.

Did you know?

You can double-click the task from the To-do bar or the Tasks view.

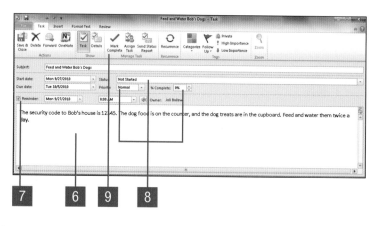

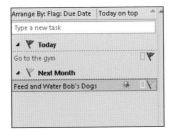

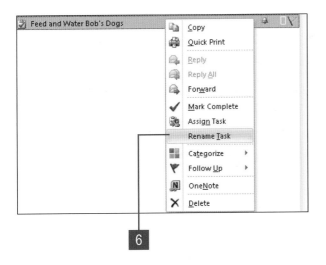

Tasks (cont.)

Manage tasks

1 Enter Task view.

2 Select any task by clicking it once.

3 From the Home tab, notice that you can:

   a Delete the task.

   b Forward the task.

   c Mark it complete.

4 Click the View tab.

5 Click Change View.

6 In the Task List, right-click any task to rename it, among other things.

13

Stay organised and be efficient

Introduction

You can acquire an Inbox full of email just as easily as you can acquire a curio cabinet full of knickknacks, a garage full of rubbish or a drawer full of junk. You may be unsure why you keep so much of it and what significance it holds. You may spend more time working around these items than you do appreciating or using them, too. That's why, in this chapter, we'll focus on getting and keeping your Inbox clean, first and foremost.

Once you understand how to manage what's in your Inbox, to maintain a clean Inbox for the long term you'll have to create folders and subfolders to manage your mail. You can't leave everything in your Inbox you need to save; it'd get pretty cluttered. The more you work with email the more you'll have to save, too. You may find you keep receipts, maps and even long email conversations so you can access them later. With a clean Inbox you'll then learn how to further manage your mail by creating rules and colour-coding and flagging what's important.

There are a few things you can do to get even more from Outlook, though, like using the Outlook Today view and Conversation view. You can search for email you can't find using the Search window and create your own Search Folders to manage your mail even better. You should also learn to delete emails that pile up in your Sent and Deleted email folders, to maintain Outlook and have a basic strategy for backing up your Outlook data. The most important thing to take from this chapter is that you have to *maintain* Outlook – just as you'd maintain a file cabinet, junk drawer, or even a home, and that you can get more from Outlook by using various views and features.

The fewer emails you have in your Inbox, the better. The only emails that should be in your Inbox are those that need attention and any you haven't had time to read or reply to. For instance, you may have a flyer for the community centre to edit, a gardening question from a friend you've yet to find an answer to, or an estimate from a repair shop you'd like to compare to others you're expecting.

Take a look at your Inbox and ask yourself the following questions:

- Can I delete this email? Have I dealt with it appropriately?

- Is this a receipt, estimate or invoice I need to print and permanently file? If so, can I delete it once I've done that? Although we all want to be 'green' and watch how much paper we use, and we'd like to save money by not printing anything unnecessarily, it's okay to print important documents you receive in an email and file them (in case something happens to your computer).

- Is this email really so funny or interesting that I can't delete it?

- If I can't delete the email now, when can I? What do I need to do before I can delete it?

- If I were to create folders in Outlook to manage the emails I want to keep, what would the names of those folders be? (Taxes, Doctors, Insurance Information, Boating, Travel, Languages, Work, etc.)

We understand that you can't delete everything in your Inbox and that there are some things you do need to keep. To keep order then, you'll create email folders for those items and move them into the new folders regularly. Spend some time really thinking about the things you want to save and write down a list of potential folder names. Then see if you can 'stack' any of those to further streamline Outlook. For instance, you could create a folder named Outdoor Activities and have subfolders under that named Boating, Gardening and Soccer. Here's how Outlook is organised on my computer.

Keep your inbox clean

14

Keep your inbox clean (cont.)

Create subfolders

1. Right-click Personal Folders and click New Folder.

2. Type a name for the folder.

3. Select the 'parent' folder. The folder you are creating will appear underneath the item you select.

4. Click OK.

5. Note the new folder in the left pane of Outlook.

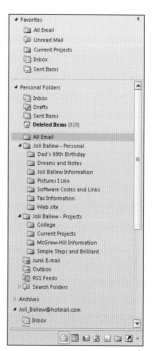

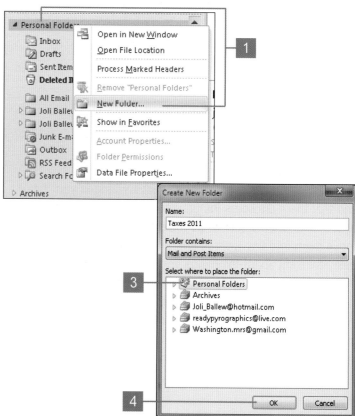

Timesaver tip

Click Personal Folders, as shown in the figure, when creating your first folder and it will appear under the Personal Folders heading shown in Step 1, above. Later you can create subfolders under folders you've created.

Now that you've created a folder it's easy to move email into it. You simply drag an email from its current folder to the appropriate folder. You can drag email from any folder to any other folder. (Even from Deleted Items to your Inbox!) Remember, though, to move an email you have to hold down the left mouse key while dragging and let it go once you're hovering over the folder you want to move it to.

Now that you have a single folder under Personal Folders, you can create additional folders and subfolders for them. You can create additional parent folders named Sports, Retirement and Hobbies before moving on. Go ahead and do that now and when you're ready, we'll move on to creating subfolders for those folders.

Once you've created all of the parent folders you need, create subfolders for them. Under Sports, you could create Soccer, Gardening and Golfing, for instance. In our example, under our Taxes folder we might create subfolders named House, Land, Health, Income and Miscellaneous. To create a subfolder you perform the same series of steps for creating a parent folder, except when creating the subfolder you first expand the Personal Folders list by clicking the triangle, then click the desired parent folder, such as Sports. In our case, that would be Taxes (vs. Personal Folders, as we did earlier).

Move mail into subfolders

1 Select the email to move.

2 While holding down the left mouse button, drag the email to the folder you want to move it to.

3 Let go to drop it into the folder.

14

Keep your inbox clean (cont.)

If at any point you do not like the folder system you've created, you have lots of choices. You can drag a folder or subfolder to another area of the Navigation pane to reposition and re-categorise it. You might decide Health should not be a subfolder of Taxes and instead be a folder of its own, a parent folder. To make this change, drag the folder to Personal Folders. It will reappear in the list there. Of course, you can drag any folder to any other folder. If you wanted to move Health to the Sports folder, for instance, you could.

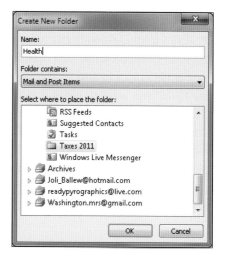

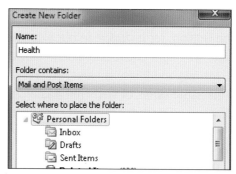

You can also rename or delete any folder by right-clicking it. If you create folders for temporary projects or one-off events, such as remodelling a home or going on holiday, it's easy to delete those once you no longer need them. When the project or event is complete, you may also decide to move it to another folder to archive it (such as Completed Projects or All Travel). It's your filing system and you can do what you want!

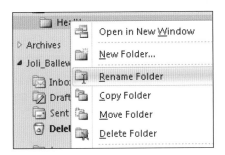

?

Did you know?

When you move a folder into another folder it becomes a subfolder. When a folder has subfolders, an arrow appears beside it. Click the arrow to show or hide the subfolders.

14

Use Outlook Views

Explore Outlook Today

1 Click Personal Folders.

2 Review what's shown in Outlook Today.

3 Click Customize Outlook Today.

Outlook has more views and more features that you've yet to explore. There's the Outlook Today view and there's Folder view. These views offer daily summary information and access to all Outlook has to offer, including Calendar, Contacts, Tasks and Notes. We'll encourage you to explore these views in the upcoming sections. You should also look briefly at a new view, Conversation view, if you have long conversations with others via email. Conversation view lets you hide unwanted copies of past emails to streamline what you see in your Inbox.

Let's start with Outlook Today. You access Outlook Today by clicking Personal Folders in the Navigation pane. It may not have much to show, as you can see here. However, you can customise it so that it shows specific folders, opens to this view when you start Outlook and more.

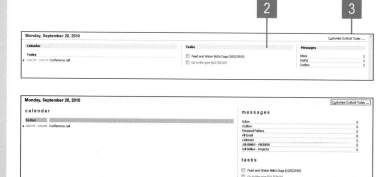

If you opt to use this view, you can quickly see today's calendar appointments, tasks and messages and are able to obtain a summary of your schedule before heading to your Inbox.

There's another view to explore, and it's called Folder View. You may have noticed the folder icon at the bottom of the Navigation pane when you explored the Calendar, Contacts, Tasks and Notes options in Chapter 13. Unlike those views which focus solely on the feature, Folder view enables you to access all of the features in Outlook from a single view. Here's Folder view. Note the access to Inbox, Calendar, Contacts, Tasks and Notes, all from a single pane.

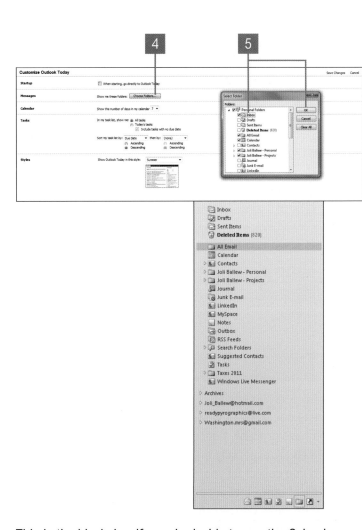

4 Click Choose Folders.

5 Select the folders to display and click OK.

6 Configure other options as desired.

7 Click Save Changes.

This is the ideal view if you do decide to use the Calendar, Contacts, Notes and Tasks features regularly. With a single click you can access limited views of these features. For instance, if you click Calendar, you can view your calendar but you won't have the advanced options accessible to you. You may notice similar limitations with other features. However, for the most part you don't need access to the advanced tools, you only need to see your calendar and be able to create and edit appointments, view your contacts and select one, or view your tasks and note your progress.

Important

We've installed a few Outlook add-ons, so our Navigation pane will likely look different from yours.

14

Use Outlook Views (cont.)

Use the Folder view

1 Click the Folder view icon at the bottom of the Navigation pane.

2 Click Inbox, then click Contacts, Calendar and Tasks.

3 To return to Mail view or any other, click the appropriate icon at the bottom of the Navigation pane.

To complete our study of views, we'll end with Conversation view. You have probably noticed as you 'converse' with people via email, especially if there's a lot of back-and-forth, the emails you collect fill your Inbox quickly. You can reduce the amount of email that appears in your Inbox by turning on Conversation view. Conversation view groups and sorts your email by conversation, helping you keep your Inbox organised.

While in Conversation view, you can sort email by Date, From, To and various other options, just as you can in any other view. And you can use the Clean Up command from the Home tab to 'clean up' conversations you have with others. Clean Up automatically keeps the most recent messages and discards unnecessary ones, thus making keeping up with the latest updates to the conversation simple. It will not discard attachments, flagged emails or categories, so it's safe to use, too.

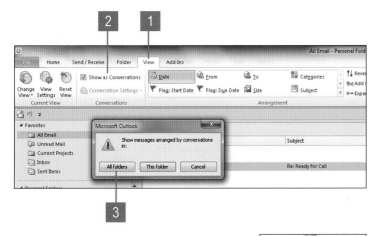

Use Outlook Views (cont.)

Explore Conversation View

1. Click the View tab.
2. Check Show As Conversations.
3. Opt to apply to all folders.
4. To expand or minimise a conversation, click the triangle.

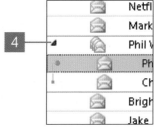

14

While in Conversation view, all back-and-forth emails between you and another person (or group of people) will appear with a triangle beside it. Click the most recent email to view the latest update to the conversation or to view all emails in the conversation thread.

Flag, categorise and manage email

Flag email

1 Select any email to flag.

2 Click Follow Up on the Home tab.

3 Choose when to follow up. If you opt for Custom, you'll have the option to configure additional settings:

  a Apply a name for the follow up.

  b To create a reminder.

  c To set a specific date and time.

4 Note the new flag in the To-do bar.

Beyond the additional views you've explored thus far, there are options to flag and colour-code emails to further manage them. By flagging an email you can add a note about it in your Tasks list in the To-do pane. This should help you remember to deal with the item within the allotted time frame. You can flag an email and be reminded about it today, tomorrow, this week, next week or any date you select. You can even configure a reminder to appear in the form of a sound and pop-up, so there will be no mistaking the item is an important one. By colour-coding your emails you have the opportunity to organise them by assigning each a certain colour. Perhaps you'll use green for your gardening club, blue for your swimming club and yellow for emails from your grandchildren.

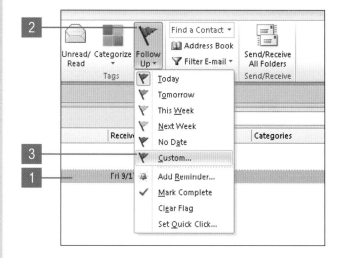

Once you have flagged items in the to-do bar, you can click them once to have access to the Task Tools, click them twice to open the Task window, or right-click to see additional options such as Mark Complete, Categorize and Follow Up. All of these options should look familiar to you; the Tasks Tools tab is just another tab with options; the Task window looks like the familiar Appointment or Event window; the right-click options look just like any other as well.

As mentioned before, another option for managing email is to colour-code messages. There are multiple ways to colour-code (or categorise) an email, but the easiest is to either right-click it or select Categorize from the Home tab, shown here. You also have the option to rename any category. For instance, if you do decide that the Green category will be used to designate email from your gardening club, you can rename it that. You can access the option to rename a category, whose dialogue box is shown here, by clicking All Categories under the Categories list, also shown.

Flag, categorise and manage email (cont.)

Important

If you need to follow up on an email at a later date but are afraid you'll forget, flag it. For instance, if you need to check on the status of a possible job opening, verify you've received contracts in the post, or check the status of an order that is supposed to ship a week from today, you can create a flag to remind you to check in or check back at that time.

14

Flag, categorise and manage email (cont.)

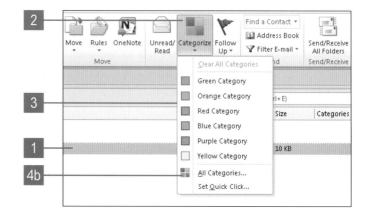

Apply a colour category

1 Select any email to categorise it.

2 From the Home tab, click Categorize.

3 Select a category colour.

4 To rename a category:

  a Click Categorize again.

  b Click All Categories.

  c Click any category to rename.

  d Click Rename.

  e Type the new name.

  f Click OK.

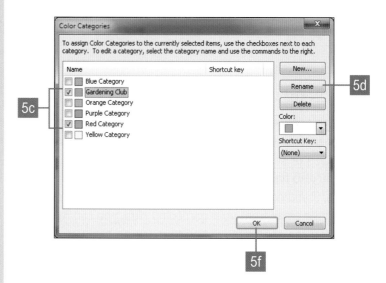

After you've applied a category it will appear on the email itself along with any other items you've added, such as any follow-up notifications. You can then sort emails by their colour and easily search for emails that are important (marked in Red perhaps), emails regarding an upcoming holiday (Blue perhaps), or emails to do with a new hobby (Purple, perhaps).

Additionally, you can click Categories in Outlook's Inbox to sort items there by their categories. Once you're finished with this view, to return to the default view, click Received. (Note that you can click Name to sort the email in the list by names, or by other column titles.)

?

Did you know?

You can apply colour categories to almost anything in Outlook, including Contacts, Calendar appointments and Events, Tasks and Notes. Once applied, as with email, you can sort and manage these items by their colour.

14

Search and search folders

Outlook has three search folders built-in: Categorized Mail, Large Mail and Unread Mail. This allows you to quickly access mail you've previously categorised, mail that contains large attachments (such as a PDF for an estimate for a caravan remodel) or mail you've yet to read.

Outlook also comes with a Search window, where you can type a keyword and search all of your mail items for something specific. This is a good way to find a missing or lost email, especially if you can remember something very specific about it.

Finally, you can create your own search folders based on criteria you set. You may want to create a search folder that contains copies of all of the email you received from a specific person, containing a specific word or to a specific group of people.

Let's start by expanding the Search Folders option in the Navigation pane. To expand the folder to show its subfolders, click the triangle beside it. You should be able to see the folders shown here. Click any folder to see its contents. It's important to note that the items you see in this folder (and other Search folders you will create) aren't 'copied' or moved here, and yet you don't have two copies of email on your computer either. Search Folders only offers access to these emails. Emails will still appear in all the other places you expect them to.

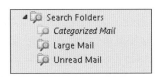

There is an option in Outlook to search for an email using a keyword. To do this, you type the keyword into the window and the results will be shown below it. The more specific you can be about your search the better. If you search for your name, for instance, almost every email you've ever sent will appear, likely because your name will appear at the end of every email you send! It's far better to search for something more specific, like a word that isn't very common or doesn't appear in your emails very often.

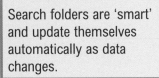

Did you know?

Search folders are 'smart' and update themselves automatically as data changes.

If Outlook can't find what you need it may prompt you to look in 'All Email'. If prompted, do so. As you can see here, if the item exists, Outlook will find it.

!	⌂	◻	ⓘ	From	▼	Subject	Received	Size	Categories	Outlook Data File
▲ From: Joli Ballew (6 items)										
				Joli Ballew			Wed 5/19/2010 11:07 AM	2 MB		Personal Folders
				Joli Ballew		86304c_JB	Mon 5/17/2010 1:23 PM	47...		Personal Folders
!				Joli Ballew		FW: How to Do EverythingT: iPadT- schedule and Chapter ...	Mon 5/17/2010 1:03 PM	22...		Personal Folders
				Joli Ballew		FW: Chapter 4	Tue 5/11/2010 3:47 PM	89...		Personal Folders
				Joli Ballew		Rules for Bocce	Tue 5/4/2010 2:23 PM	5 KB		Personal Folders
				Joli Ballew		Chapter 4 iPad	Tue 5/4/2010 1:05 PM	46 ...		Personal Folders

Rules for Bocce
Joli Ballew <Joli_Ballew@txrr.com>
Sent: Tue 5/4/2010 2:23 PM
To: 'Joli Ballew'

Here are the rules for the outdoor game, Bocce. Have a great picnic!

Sometimes you'll need to find more than a single email. In this case, the default Search folders – Categorized, Unread and Large – don't fit the bill. If you ever need to gather multiple emails together that relate to a single subject that you'd like to define, you can try to amass those emails by creating your own search folder.

To expand on our previous search for Bocce, this time we'll create a Search folder that will gather all of the emails with the word Bocce in it, and we'll save the results in a Search folder named Bocce. Remember that emails aren't moved there, though, and copies are not made. Only access is granted to them from a single folder. You may want to consider creating a search folder to hold emails you receive from a group or club, like a golf league or knitting club.

14

Search and search folders (cont.)

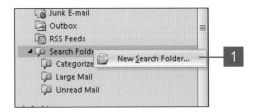

Create a Search Folder

1. Right-click Search Folders and click New Search Folder.

2. For this example, scroll down and click Mail with Specific Words.

3. Click Choose.

4. Type the words to search for, click Add, then click OK.

5. Click OK.

6. Notice the new search folder in the Search Folders list.

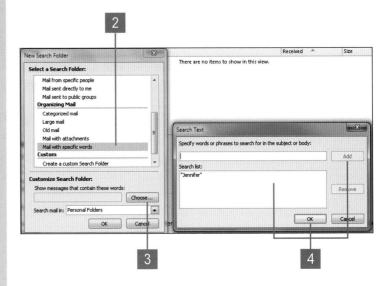

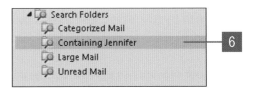

Emails collect in the corners and crevasses of Outlook in places you might not think, similar to how cobwebs collect in doorways and corners when you're not looking. There are two main hiding places for emails; all emails you send are saved in the Sent folder, and all emails you delete are saved in the Deleted Items folder. After a year or so, you can imagine how this would build up!

In order to maintain Outlook, you must occasionally delete the items in these folders. You can do that in several ways, but we prefer to select the folder in the Navigation pane and delete all but the last 3 months of emails. If you agree that you'd like to keep some of the emails, click the Sent folder and then click Sent to order the emails by the date you sent them. Then, choose the emails to delete by selecting them while holding down the Shift key or the Ctrl key. Once selected, you can right-click and choose Delete.

Sent ▲	Size	Categories	⫶
Mon 9/20/20...	25 KB		
Mon 9/20/20...	26 KB		
Tue 9/21/201...	32 KB		
Tue 9/21/201...	5 KB		
Tue 9/21/201...	33 KB		
Tue 9/21/201...	6 KB		

? Did you know?

When you delete items in the Sent folder they go to the Deleted Items folder. Thus, it's best to empty items in Sent first, and then empty items in Deleted Items next.

It's much easier to delete everything in the Sent or Deleted Items folders. You can do this with a right-click.

14

Maintaining Outlook (cont.)

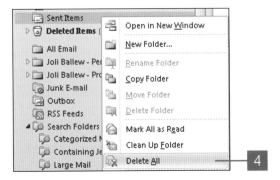

Delete email

1 Click the folder that contains emails to delete.

2 Select the emails to delete.

3 Right-click the selected items, then click Delete.

4 Alternatively, right click Sent or Deleted Items and click Delete All to empty the folder.

Create a rule for incoming email

1 Select any email you'd like to base the new rule on.

2 From the Home tab, click Rules.

3 Click Create Rule.

For your information

Remember, you can select multiple, contiguous emails by holding down the Shift key while selecting. To select non-contiguous, use Ctrl.

Another way to maintain Outlook is to create rules for email. Outlook lets you create rules for just about any purpose imaginable. You can create a rule that automatically filters email from a specific person to a specific folder (for instance, all email from a grandchild to a folder called Grandchild, or all email from a doctor to a folder called Doctor). You can create rules to block email that contains specific words you don't like, too, or even send an alert to your mobile phone when you receive an email from a specific person, among other things.

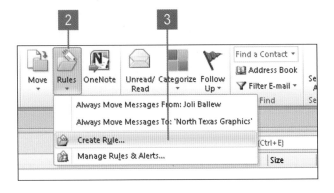

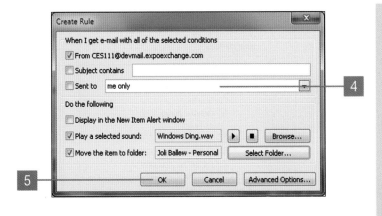

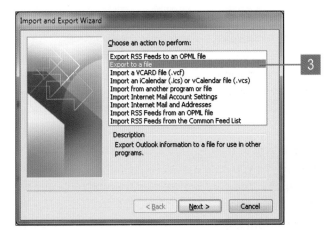

4 Configure the rule as desired.

5 Click OK.

6 To test the rule, click Run this rule now on messages already in the current folder, when prompted, and click OK.

Back up Outlook data

1 Click File and click Open.

2 Click Import.

3 In the Import and Export Wizard, click Export to a File.

14

Finally, you need to know how to back up Outlook data. Your Outlook data is stored in a personal folder file. In order to keep that data safe, you should back it up regularly. We suggest weekly. When you work through the backup process here, though, make sure you follow the directions step-by-step. You want to back up all your folders, including Contacts, Calendar, Tasks and Notes, and all of their subfolders. You'll also want to move or copy that backup to an external entity, such as a DVD, external drive or flash drive for safe keeping.

?

Did you know?

You can create a new rule from scratch; just click Rules and click Manage Rules and Alerts. Click New Rule to get started.

Maintaining Outlook (cont.)

4 Click Next.

5 Click Outlook Data File (.pst).

6 Click Next.

7 Click Personal Folder, and check Include subfolders.

8 Click Next.

9 Click Browse.

10 Locate a place to store the backup. Click OK.

11 Make a choice regarding duplicates.

12 Click Finish.

13 If desired, create a password.

14 Click OK.

15 Move the backup, if applicable, to an external drive, flash drive, network drive, CD or DVD.

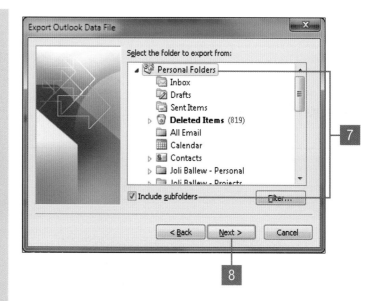

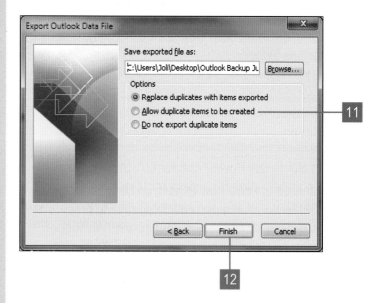

PowerPoint basics

Introduction

Microsoft Office PowerPoint is a powerful presentation-making program that is often used in business to enhance an oral presentation. If you give presentations to clients, bosses, community leaders, associations or committees, this may be just what you need to make your point, seal the deal, get that contribution or make the sale. You can also use PowerPoint to create slideshows that run in the background while potential viewers do something else. You can create a presentation to run a product demo at a kiosk, or use a presentation to show activity schedules, lunch schedules or agenda information, where applicable.

You may prefer to use PowerPoint for fun, though. You can create a presentation for a class reunion, retirement party or birthday party, and include old pictures, quotes and animations. You can create a slideshow of your children and grandchildren and use it as a type of screensaver on your computer. And just as you can with other Office programs, you can choose from all kinds of templates to help you get the job done quickly and easily.

What you'll do

Explore Templates

Create slides

Add text and additional slides

Add pictures and clip art

Edit slide content

Add pizzazz

> **!**
>
> ## Important
>
> If you use a digital photo frame to display family photos, you probably won't be able to show a PowerPoint presentation on it. Keep that in mind. You'll need a computer to present what you create in this chapter.

Explore Templates

Templates give you a starting point for your presentation or project. As with Word and Excel, there are lots of templates to choose from. You'll find templates for entire presentations, of course, but also for award certificates, calendars, single slides, photo albums and more. Thus, PowerPoint can not only act as presentation-creation software, it can also serve as a sort of desktop publishing program, enabling you to create things like certificates and calendar pages that you can print and share easily. If you do opt to create a presentation, you'll want to show it too; you can do that with PowerPoint as well. You can even connect to an external projector; it's all built right in!

As we've done elsewhere in this book, we'll encourage you to look at the available templates before starting any project. And as we've said before, it's because there's no reason to reinvent the wheel every time you want to create something. Why spend three hours creating the perfect slide, complete with a background, text boxes, picture place holders and specific fonts with their own font qualities when you can select a template that already has what you need built right in?

Important

While exploring templates you may encounter a message stating that a particular template category is no longer available, or you may see additional categories you won't see in the screen shots here. This is because Microsoft is continually updating the templates to offer the best and most appropriate templates for its PowerPoint users, and thus what's available from Office.com changes regularly.

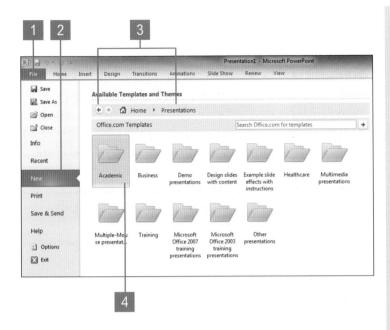

Explore Templates

1. Click the File tab.

2. Click New to view the template categories.

3. Click Presentations and drill into any category (use the back arrow to return to a previous screen.)

4. Double-click any template to download it.

Important

The templates from the New tab of the File menu come from Office.com, which is an online resource. You have to be connected to the Internet to access them.

Regarding templates, as you explore consider the following:

- You don't have to purchase a calendar or planner when you can create one yourself. There are plenty of templates that make it easy. What's great about creating your own calendar is that you can add clip art and input events on their respective calendar boxes before printing it, and even share the calendar via email, print, post or by publishing it to a web page.

- Professional wedding invitations are expensive. It's all the rage among the young people these days to print your own and save money. Being frugal is hip. Invitations printed at home can look almost as good as those printed professionally, too, provided you print on fancy paper and use a decent enough printer.

- The older you get, the more announcements you have to make! There are 60th, 70th, 80th and 90th birthdays, the birth of grandchildren and great-grandchildren, graduations, awards and retirement parties. Spend less time creating announcements and more time celebrating by creating the announcements using templates.

Explore
Templates (cont.)

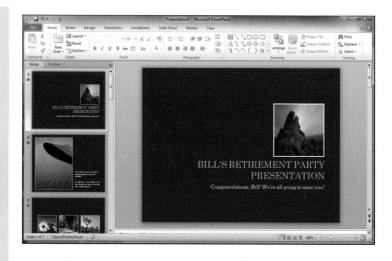

Once you've selected a template you can practise moving around in it and reviewing what's available from the PowerPoint interface. You'll see familiar offerings. There are tabs on the Ribbon, just like with other Office programs, and when you click any tab the items on the Ribbon change to reflect your choice. As with other Office applications, there are tab groups that contain tools that are similar, so you can easily find what you want. And, when you click any element in any slide (such as a text box, picture or table), a new tab appears that contains tools for working with it. (You'll have to click the tab to access the tools under it.)

Did you know?

You can reposition the panes by dragging from the separators between them.

Notice what's called out in this image, including the Notes pane, Status Bar, Zoom Slider and other items. Beyond that, here are a few other things to explore:

- Slides and Outline views – in the Slides view in the left pane, click any slide. The selected slide will appear in the Current Slide pane. Initially, you'll work in Slides view. There, you can drag and drop slides to rearrange them, or click to view them.

- Formatting options on the Home tab – click inside any text box to show the familiar formatting options.

- Insert tab – click to insert pictures, shapes, clip art and other items.

- Design tab – click to add a theme to the entire presentation with a single click.

Did you know?

The Transitions tab enables you to select how one slide changes to another by fading in, cutting in, pushing in and more.

Create slides

Slides are the building blocks of any presentation. All presentations have slides. Slides contain text, pictures, bulleted and numbered lists and other elements. Once you've created all of the slides for a presentation you can play it, present it, turn it on and let it loop and more. If you'd like to add additional elements after saving and viewing your presentation, you can do that too. You can add transitions to enhance how one slide 'moves' into the next, you can add animations and you can even add sound.

Jargon buster

Slides – slides are the building blocks of every PowerPoint presentation. You may recall that in the 'olden days' you'd place and order 35mm physical slides in a slide sorter/presenter to create a slide presentation. These days you create virtual slides in PowerPoint.

You'll want to be adept at working with slides, since they are the basis for all of your presentations. Beyond creating them by adding the elements you need, it's also important you know how to hide slides, add additional slides, delete slides, copy slides and move slides, among other things. We'll try to cover all of that here, in a single chapter, to get you up to speed quickly with PowerPoint.

Text and pictures are the mainstays of any slide. Text is often formatted in bullets and numbered lists, although short paragraphs and quotations are certainly acceptable material. Throughout this chapter you'll learn how to work with text as well as pictures and how to move those elements around in any slide you create.

In this example we'll start with a Family Reunion template and input pictures and information about an event we've already held. When the presentation is complete, we'll email it to all of the reunion attendees, as a remembrance of the day. You should feel free to choose any template you like; you'll be able to work alongside our examples no matter which template you select.

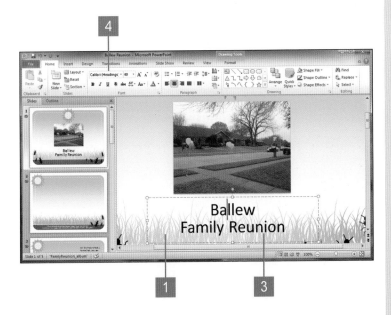

To get started, click inside any slide that offers a place to input text, as shown here, and type the text that's appropriate for your project. If you're using a template, the best place to start is the first slide. There's almost always boilerplate text you can click and replace to use as a title. You'll input text the same way you'd input text in any other program, by clicking and typing. Note when typing that formatting tools are available from the Home tab, enabling you to select fonts, font colours and more.

Add text and additional slides

Insert text into an existing text box

1 Click inside any text box.

2 Select any existing text by dragging the mouse over it, if applicable.

3 Type the desired text.

4 Format the text as desired.

15

Add text and additional slides (cont.)

It's important to understand that text in PowerPoint is input into a 'text box', also shown. This is quite a bit different from what you may be used to when typing in Word, Excel or Outlook. Text boxes are necessary with PowerPoint so that you can place the text box (and thus the text) anywhere you like on any given slide. When a text box is selected, you can drag from the centre or corners to resize and reshape the text box easily.

You can also insert a text box into any slide manually, an option available from the Insert tab. When you do this, you design the text box, the font, the font size and other text attributes.

Important

Remember to click the File tab and click Save As to save the file before continuing.

As with any Microsoft Office program you can use familiar editing tools:

- Use Cut, Copy and Paste – select the data to be cut or copied. Right-click the selected data. Click Cut or Copy. Place the mouse cursor where you'd like to paste the cut or copied data, right-click and select Paste.

- Use the Mini Toolbar – select the text to format. Right-click it. Choose the desired formatting from the Mini Toolbar.

- Add bulleted or numbered lists – from the Home tab, select the list type. Type the list, pressing Enter or Return on the keyboard after each entry.

- Use Undo Typing and Redo Typing – type anything. Click the Undo Typing button on the toolbar to remove it. To undo multiple entries, click the arrow next to Undo Typing and select how many entries to undo.To redo typing, click the Redo Typing button next to Undo Typing.

- Use Find and Replace – from the Home tab, click Replace. Type the information to find and the information to replace it with. To replace all entries quickly, click Replace All. You'll be notified regarding the changes.

- Use the Format Painter – select the data that contains formatting to copy. Click Format Painter on the Home tab. Click the desired location to apply the formatting.

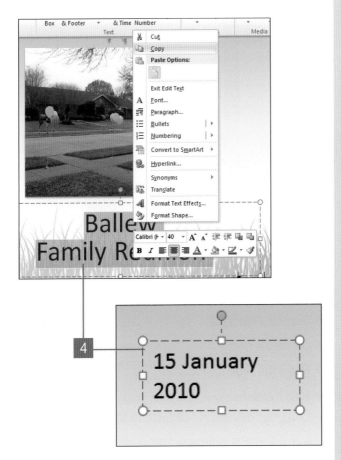

Insert your own text box

1. On any slide, click the Insert tab.

2. Click Text Box.

3. Click and drag with the cursor to create the box.

4. Type the desired text.

Did you know?

The green circle at the top of a text box enables you to rotate the box.

15

Add text and additional slides (cont.)

When you open a new, blank presentation, there's one slide available and it's blank. If you've selected a template, there may be one or several slides, and they'll already have some formatting. No matter what's the case, though, if you're working on a presentation from scratch or from a template, you'll likely need to insert additional slides.

Create a new slide

1 Right-click any slide and click New Slide to insert a slide after it.

or

2 From the Home tab, click New Slide, and select the type of slide to add.

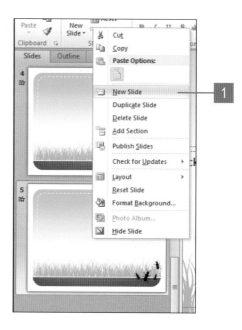

Before continuing, take a look at the other options available by right-clicking a slide. While we won't go into all of these in the remaining space we have, it's easy to deduce how to use these options. Among other things, you can:

- Duplicate the slide.
- Delete the slide.
- Reset the slide.
- Hide the slide.

Click the desired choice to perform the desired task. After you've inserted a slide you may want to change the slide layout.

A picture is worth a thousand words, and a picture is the best way to describe what 'slide layout' is. In this figure you can see several slide layout options. Note the first slide layout, 'Album Cover', contains only a place for a picture and a title. Note the last slide layout option, 'Blank' only has the background. (If you wanted to add text here, you'd have to add your own text box.) In the centre of the options are several that have picture placeholders and a place for text, including 3-Up Portrait with Captions and 2-Up Landscape with Captions. You can change any slide layout by right-clicking it.

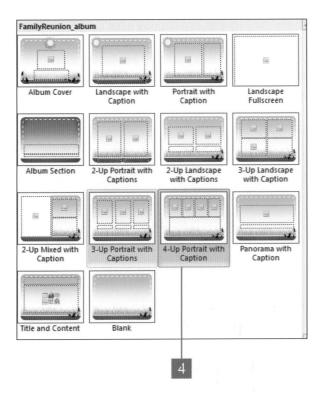

Change the slide layout

1 Create a new slide or select an existing one.

2 Right-click the slide.

3 Click Layout.

4 Select the desired slide.

Add pictures and clip art

Insert a picture

1 If there's an option to 'click here' or 'click icon' to add a picture, click it.

You'll almost always want to insert pictures or clip art when creating slides. You may use a picture of a product for a business presentation, a picture of a person for a birthday party slideshow or a picture from a vacation for a personal photo album. Beyond what *you* want to convey, though, it's important your presentation has slides to keep *your audience* engaged. Text alone just won't cut it, even if you add fancy bullets and lists. Don't worry, adding pictures in PowerPoint is just as simple as adding pictures in Word or Outlook; it's a breeze.

There are various ways to insert a picture, and we'll discuss them briefly here so you can choose what's right for you:

■ If you're working from a template you may see instructions to 'click icon' or 'click here' to replace an existing picture or placeholder icon. Click this to add a picture.

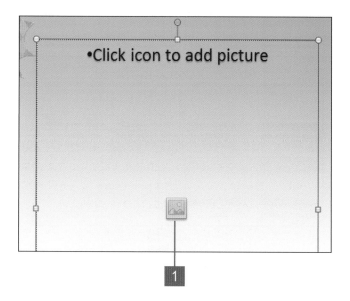

■ You can right-click any picture placeholder to access the insertion options, namely, Change Picture.

■ You can insert a picture into a blank slide (or any other) by using the Insert tab. From there you'll find the option to insert not only pictures, but clip art, shapes, SmartArt and more.

2 If there is a picture placeholder and no option to 'click here', right-click it and select Change Picture.

3 Browse to the location of the picture to add and select it.

4 Click Insert.

It's important to note that when you start from a picture placeholder in a template or from a slide with a layout that includes a picture placeholder, for the most part the picture you select will be automatically resized so it will fit in the allotted place on the slide. This is quite convenient and very effective. If you start with a blank slide, though, and use the Insert tab, the picture is not resized to fit in any particular area of the slide, which means you have to do it manually, by dragging from the corners of the picture.

So, before you start adding pictures and clip art, create your slide first then select a slide layout that already has the desired number of picture placeholders. It's just easier to work from here, especially if *Click icon to add picture* is available.

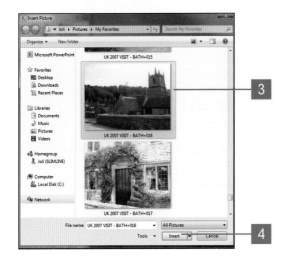

15

Add pictures and clip art (cont.)

Did you know?

After inserting a picture a new tab will appear, Picture Tools, which will enable you to edit the picture.

Clip art is digital art you obtain from various third parties on disks and online. Office comes with its own clip art, available from Office.com. You can search the clip art library to find the perfect graphic for your needs. As with other Office programs, you'll use the Insert tab to insert clip art. From the Insert tab, click Clip Art and locate the art to add.

You already know how to replace, format and edit text. In PowerPoint, though, there's more to it than that. Since everything is in a 'box' of some sort, you can easily move the content to another area of a slide, or to a completely different slide. You do this by dragging the box. Here we're simply repositioning the picture to the top left of the slide instead of the bottom middle.

If you know that when you're presenting your PowerPoint presentation you're going to want to click a link in a slide and go to a website, you'll need to add a hyperlink. A hyperlink offers a way to quickly access a page on the Internet; you have probably encountered them in emails and while surfing the web. When you click a hyperlink in a slide, your web browser opens and the page is accessed (provided you're online). Hyperlinks are also useful if you're sending a presentation in an email, because the recipient will likely be watching the presentation on their own computer and will have the option to click the hyperlink to visit your website. You add a hyperlink by selecting the text to apply the hyperlink to and selecting Hyperlink.

 Edit slide content

Move and resize content

1. Position the cursor towards the top of the box to move.

2. When the four-headed arrow appears, click and drag the box to its new position.

3. Drop the box there to complete the move.

15

Edit slide content (cont.)

Insert a hyperlink

1 To add a hyperlink to text, an image, SmartArt or other item, first select the item.

2 Right-click the item.

3 Click Hyperlink.

4 Type, paste or browse to the location of the website.

5 Click OK.

For your information

When you add a hyperlink to text, the text becomes underlined to denote this. If you add a hyperlink to a picture, nothing happens.

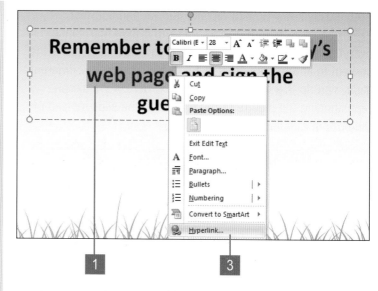

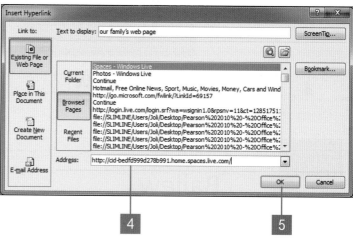

With multiple slides created and your presentation taking shape, it's time to add a little pizzazz. It's time to experiment with themes, transitions and animations, among other things. You access these features from the various tabs on PowerPoint's Ribbon.

Themes are all-encompassing and can really change the look of a presentation quickly. A theme is a group of elements that include background colours, graphics and preconfigured fonts, font sizes and matching font colours. You can apply a theme after you've finished inputting your text, pictures and other data, or you can create a presentation quickly and easily by selecting a theme right at the beginning. You select themes from the Design tab.

Select any slide in your presentation, preferably one with at least a couple of elements like text and pictures, and from the Design tab, hover your mouse over the available themes in the Themes group. You can preview how the themes would look on your presentation. To apply a new theme, click it. Note you can access more themes by clicking the down arrow in the Themes group.

Add pizzazz

Important

You can change the theme at any time, even after inputting text and images, and your data will remain intact (although its position, size and features may change to incorporate the new theme's characteristics).

Important

If you have trouble matching colours and fonts, or don't consider yourself the creative type, work from a theme.

15

Add pizzazz (cont.)

Apply a theme

1. Open a new, blank PowerPoint presentation.

2. Click the Design tab.

3. Hover the mouse over the available themes to see their previews, and then click the arrow in the Themes group to see all of the options.

4. Click any theme to apply it.

? **Did you know?**

When you apply a theme, it will be applied to any new slides you create for the current presentation.

When you play your presentation as a slide show, by default there is no 'transition' when you move from slide to slide. One slide simply disappears and the next appears. You can apply a transition so that one slide dissolves into another, slips in from the left or the right, dissolves in and out, or even pans in. We think it's always good to apply at least a few transitions between at least a few slides; it gives the presentation pizzazz.

You access transitions from the Transitions tab, as you've probably guessed. As you explore this option, notice that you can also add a sound to the transition, add transition effects (which are variations on the transition), apply the transition you select to all slides in the presentation and even opt to have the slide change automatically after a certain number of seconds. All of this is made available to you with easy-to-use check boxes and drop-down lists, something you're probably by now quite comfortable with.

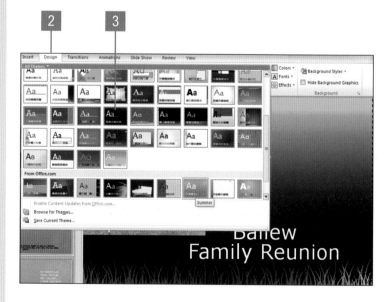

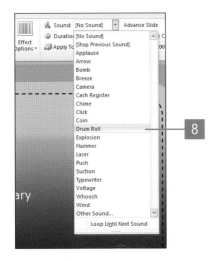

Important

!

To advance slides automatically for a presentation you do not want to manage, such as one at a kiosk, class reunion or retirement party, remove the check by Advance Slide, On Mouse Click and set a duration in the After window.

An animation is a digital, visual enhancement to a single slide. Animations enable you to have text boxes, bullets, numbered lists, pictures, clip art and such to fade in, fly in, float in and wipe in, among other things, and you can configure the 'trigger'. For instance, you may want to click to have each bullet or a bulleted list appear, so that you have time to discuss each bullet before introducing the next. Animations are kind of like transitions in that they cause 'movement' in your presentation. But with animations, you pick the element to move, such as a bullet in a list, a picture on a slide or even text in a text box. In contrast, a transition is how one slide moves to the other slide and does not affect any element that's actually on the slide.

Add transitions

1. Click the slide you would like to apply a transition to and click the Transitions tab.

2. Click any transition to preview it.

3. To make the transition last longer (or to make it shorter) adjust the Duration.

4. To see more transitions, click the down arrow in the Transitions group.

5. If you want the slides to change automatically after a specific amount of time (vs. you clicking to advance them):

   a Remove the check by On Mouse Click.

   b Place a check by After, and select a time.

6. To add a sound to the transition, click the arrow by Sound.

7. Hover the mouse over any sound to preview it.

8. Select the sound to apply.

9. To apply this transition to all slides in your presentation, click Apply to All. Otherwise, repeat for each slide that you want to have a transition.

15

Add pizzazz (cont.)

Add animations

1. In any presentation, select any item such as a picture.

2. Click the Animations tab.

3. Click an animation to apply it.

4. Note that animations, like transitions, have Effect Options. Click the down arrow to select an option, if desired.

5. To see more animations, click the arrow in the Animations group.

6. Select any animation in the list to apply it.

Preview your presentation

1. Click the Slide Show tab.

2. Click From Beginning. (Note, you can also play from the current slide.)

3. If you set the slideshow to change slides automatically, do nothing. If you did not, you have to click the mouse to switch slides.

4. To stop a presentation, click the ESC key on the keyboard.

?

Did you know?

After applying an animation a preview of it appears. If you like it, do nothing, if you don't, select another transition.

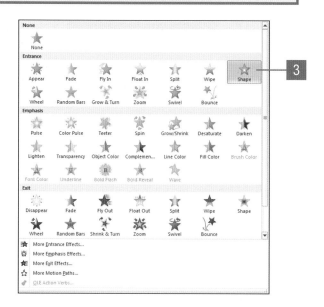

Make sure to note the other options, many of which are similar to the options in Transitions. You can choose how to start the animation (On Click is the most popular), and you can set its duration and any delay. Don't add too many animations, though; too many can be distracting.

When you think your presentation is about ready for prime time, preview it.

Create a photo album

16

Introduction

We're betting the bank that you have pictures scattered about everywhere: in your attic, in shoe boxes, on external disks and hard drives, on cameras and on memory cards. You even have photos in emails you've saved. You may have tried organising these photos before, but found the task daunting. You didn't know where to start and you didn't want to commit to a plan only to find out later it wasn't going to be what you wanted or needed. You know you need to get your old printed photos onto your computer by scanning them, and you know you need to organise those pictures in folders on your computer's hard drive (and back them up), but then what?

It's not that you're out of the loop, though; you're fully aware times have changed, especially with family photos. You understand that things aren't like they used to be; you used to just sit down with a cigar box full of printed pictures and tape them into a photo album. Perhaps, if you were feeling especially creative, you'd even write down the year and event underneath the pictures (or add captions). You know in your heart this just won't work anymore, though, even if you printed every single picture that was currently stored on your computer and tried this approach. These photo albums degenerate, can't be 'backed up' and can't be shared with your sister in Liverpool while at the same time being shared with your son in Glasgow. It's just not what you do anymore.

In this chapter you'll learn one option for managing all the photos you've so carefully amassed on your computer: Photo Album. Photo Album is a feature in PowerPoint that enables you

What you'll do

Add photos

Choose a layout and theme

Insert elements

Present and share the album

to pull photos from various sources, organise them and create a digital record of them in the form of a presentation. While creating an album you can select various layouts and themes, add captions, apply design templates, add text boxes and even display pictures in black and white, if you'd like. Of course, you don't have to do any of this! If you'd rather, you can create a simple photo album with pictures, names, dates and events, and share this with your friends and family as-is. And don't worry about compatibility, if you want to share the album with others who don't have PowerPoint, they can still view it. They just need the free PowerPoint Viewer, available from Microsoft.

!

Important

Photo Album, in this context, is not a template you get from the File tab. Photo Album is a feature available in PowerPoint 2010 from the Insert tab.

The first few steps in creating your photo album include opening the Photo Album dialogue box and selecting the photos to use in the album. Before you get started, it's imperative you decide what type of album you want to create, what pictures you want to use, and know where those pictures are located.

First, we know that you may have pictures, literally, in shoe boxes. If this is the case you'll have to scan those pictures and store them on the computer before you can use them in PowerPoint. You can buy a scanner or borrow one, and you may even be able to use a scanner at the local library. If you simply don't want the bother and have plenty of money, you can hire someone to scan all your photos and put them on a DVD as well. If you want to do it yourself, though, for the most part you place the pictures on the scanner bed or in the designated holding area, and press the appropriate button. You can crop the scanning area, as shown here, prior to scanning and apply the desired resolution, among other things. Our advice is to scan as many pictures as you can, and store them in a folder you create called Scanned Photographs in your Pictures folder on your computer.

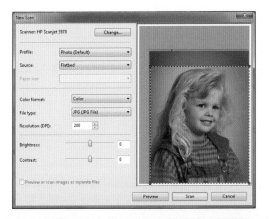

Add photos (cont.)

You may have also have pictures on your digital camera that you never uploaded to your computer. You'll need to do that before continuing. For the most part, you will insert the card into a card reader on your computer or connect your camera to an available USB port, and follow the prompts to import them. You may have pictures on a CD or DVD, or on similar media, such as external drives, thumb drives or flash drives too. You'll need to connect those drives or insert the media as applicable. If you have pictures in emails, refer to the Outlook chapters to review how to save those pictures to your hard drive. Before moving on then, go ahead and get all your ducks in a row.

When you have the pictures you want to use available from your computer, you can begin adding them into a digital photo album in PowerPoint. Just open PowerPoint, click the Insert tab, click Photo Album and click New Album to get started.

Jargon buster

Photo album – a feature of PowerPoint 2010 that enables you to create a presentation that contains your favourite pictures, complete with captions, music, titles and text and/or other elements.

After you choose to start a new Photo Album, the Photo Album dialogue box will appear where you can browse to and select each picture you want to put in the album, and you can add them individually or in groups. Initially, there won't be any pictures in the album, as shown here, and much of what's available will be greyed out. When you add your first picture, though, other areas of this dialogue box will become available, such as the picture layout and frame shape, among other things.

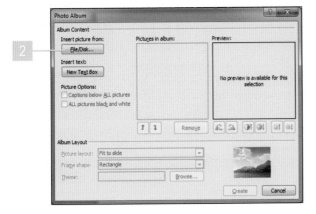

To add pictures you'll have to browse to them. This may require you to locate the pictures on your 'C:' drive, a CD/DVD drive, a USB drive, network drive or other resource. Here's what the Insert New Pictures window looks like on a Windows 7 computer, but other operating systems have different interfaces. Notice the 'path' in the top of the window. We've browsed to a computer on the network called SLIMLINE, then into a folder called Users, then Joli, then My Pictures and finally to a folder aptly called My Favorites.

Add photos from disk

1 Click Insert, Photo Album and New Photo Album.

2 Click File/Disk.

3 Browse to the location of a single picture to add.

4 To add a single picture either:

a double-click the picture to add,

or

b click it once and click Insert.

Add photos (cont.)

Although we'd prefer you edit your pictures prior to inserting them using the Photo Album, you can do a little editing once they're inserted. In the Photo Album dialogue box you can rotate an image and change its contrast and brightness. Note that you can also remove a selected picture, or move it up or down in the list of pictures in the album.

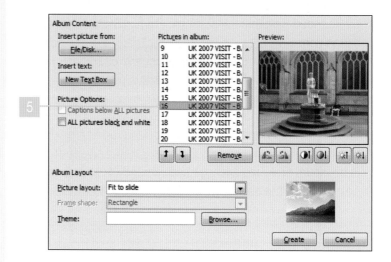

5 Note the new picture in the Pictures in Album list.

6 To insert multiple pictures at once:

a Click File/Disk again.

b Hold down the Ctrl key to select non-contiguous pictures.

Or

c Hold down the Shift key to select contiguous pictures.

d Click Insert.

7 Repeat these steps to add all of the pictures you'd like.

8 Do not click Create yet.

You know a little about slide layout from previous chapters, and while using Photo Album you have the option to apply a slide layout to your entire photo album. There are quite a few choices for Picture Layout, including Fit to Slide, 1 picture, 2 pictures, 4 pictures, 1 picture with title, 2 pictures with title and 4 pictures with title. Once you've selected that you can also apply a shape for the picture 'frame', with choice such as Rounded Rectangle and Simple Frame (Black). You can experiment with these to get a feel for them. We'll choose 1 picture with title, but feel free to select any option you like.

You can also browse and select a theme. As you know, a theme is a grouping of fonts, backgrounds, font sizes and the like, that are already configured for you. If you aren't sure about choosing a theme now, you can always create and save them in an album first, and later, go back and edit it, experimenting with available themes for them. We've chosen BlackTie.

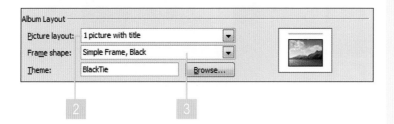

Choose an album layout and/ or theme

1 Continuing from previous sections, open the Photo Album dialogue box.

2 Under Album Layout, select a Picture layout.

3 Under Album Layout, select a Frame shape.

4 If you'd like to add a theme, click Browse by Theme, then:

   a Select the theme to use.

   b Click Select.

5 Click Create.

Create and save the album

1 In the Insert Pictures dialogue box, click Create.

2 Click the Save button on the Quick Access Toolbar.

3 Browse to the location to save the file.

4 Name the file and click Save.

Insert elements

You're now ready to complete the photo album. You may want to add text boxes, draw shapes or add clip art, which are all things you've already learned how to do. You may want to complete the text boxes inserted for you by Photo Album, which you'll have if you chose a theme that offered them, as shown here. You may decide to drag the slides in the left pane to reorder them as well. Anything you already know how to do using PowerPoint you can do now. You can even add transitions and animations! Go ahead and spend some time personalising the photo album now. When you're finished, move on to the next section.

Choose music

1 Click the Insert tab.

2 Click Audio.

3 To add audio from a file, such as a song:

   a Click Audio from File.

You can add music to a presentation from the Insert tab. There's an option to add audio; in fact, there are three options under Audio:

▦ Audio from File – to add an audio file you already have on your computer, such as a song or recording. Just about any audio file will be compatible, but you'll be notified if the file you choose is not.

- Clip Art Audio – to add audio available from the Clip Art library, including options such as Claps, Cheers, Telephone and others.

- Record Audio – to record your own audio, which is generally a narrative you add by speaking into an installed microphone on your computer.

Once you've added music, two new tabs will appear under a new tab, Audio Tools. From here you can opt to loop the music until you stop the presentation, fade in or fade out the clip or song, and even trim the audio to make it fit your slideshow exactly. You can also opt to play the music to preview it.

b Browse to the location of the file.

c Double-click the song (or file) to insert it.

4 To add clip art audio:

a Click Clip Art Audio.

b Locate the audio to add.

c Double-click the song or file to insert it.

d Note the Audio tools. You'll learn about these shortly.

Insert elements (cont.)

5 To record your own audio:

 a Click Record Audio.

 b Click the red record button in the Record Sound dialogue box.

 c Record your narration.

 d Click Stop.

 e Click OK.

6 To test any sound you've inserted, click the Play button.

7 If you don't like the audio and want to remove it, click the Undo button.

You can add video to a slide, too, although you may want to create a new slide when you do instead of adding video to a slide that already contains a picture. (Right-click any slide in the left pane and select New Slide.) With a slide ready, as with inserting music, from the Insert tab, click Video. Although there are three options for adding video, we'll only explore two here: Video from File (this is video stored on your computer), and Clip Art Video (video available from the Clip Art library from Office.com).

When you insert a video clip, the video will play when you play the slideshow and reach the slide it has been inserted into. You can preview the video in a similar manner as previewing music. You preview video from the Video Tools tab, by clicking Play. (You'll have to select the video to see these tools.)

You can't just insert any old video though. Surprisingly, some videos you take with a digital video camera and upload to your PC may not compatible. You'll have to test them and see, or view the properties for the file by right-clicking it (see the image here). However, if you try to insert a video that is not compatible, you'll get an error message saying so, so you don't have to check if you don't want to. There are five file types you can use:

▪ WMV – **Windows Media Video**

▪ AVI – **Audio Video**

- MPG or MPEG – **Moving Picture Experts Group**
- ASF – **Advanced Streaming Format**
- SWF – **Flash Video**

For your information

If you want to insert video you've taken from a digital camera and it is not stored in a compatible format, you'll have to convert it to one of these file types with third-party software.

As with inserting audio, after inserting and selecting video a new Video Tools tab will appear with two tabs under it. You can use the tools here to correct the colour in the video, change the video shape, add a video style, fade in and out, play full screen and more.

Insert elements (cont.)

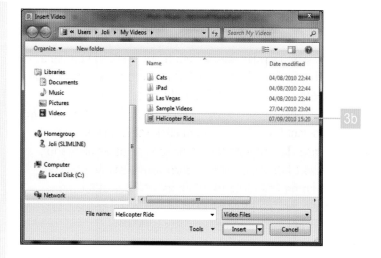

Insert a video

1 Click the Insert tab.

2 Click Video.

3 To add video from a file, such as a video you took with a digital camera:

  a Click Video from File.

  b Browse to the location of the file.

  c Double-click the song (or file) to insert it.

4 To add clip art video:

  a Click Clip Art Audio.

  b Locate the video to add.

  c Double-click the file to insert it.

  d Note the Video tools.

5 To preview any video you've inserted, click the Play button.

6 If you don't like the video and want to remove it, click the Undo button.

When you think you've finished the photo album, play it to see if you like how it turned out (use the Slide Show tab). You can then make changes as desired. If you want to choose a different theme, click Insert, click Photo Album and click Edit Photo Album. To remove slides, right-click them in the left pane and choose Delete Slide or Hide Slide. To remove music or video, select it on the slide and click the Delete key on the keyboard. To add text boxes, shapes or other elements, use the Insert tab. When you're sure you're ready, you can configure some final options, such as whether to loop the presentation instead of end it, and review your options for sharing it. Let's look at those options now.

There's an option under the Slide Show tab to Set Up Slide Show. Click this to see the Set Up Slide Show dialogue box, shown below. This is where you'll opt to loop the show continuously, as you would at a kiosk, birthday or retirement party, or in a lobby. You can also opt to show the presentation without the narration and/or animations you've added. This might be a good option if you've given the show to a crowd and then want to make the pictures and slides available to people afterwards. You can also choose the show type, which will configure many settings automatically. You can even opt to show specific slides instead of the entire photo album.

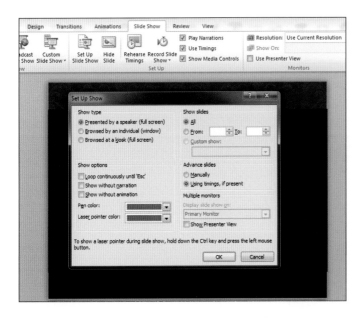

Present and share the album (cont.)

Loop the slide show

1. If you know the photo album will be viewed by an individual on their own computer, click Browsed by an individual (window).

2. If you know the photo album will be viewed at a party, click Browsed at a kiosk (full screen).

3. If you only want to show specific slides, type the sections to show in the From and To boxes.

4. If you want the show to play on its own, under Advance Slides, click Using timings, if present. If you want to click to change the slides, click Manually.

5. Click OK to apply.

You have some options for sharing your photo album. These options are available from the File tab, under Save & Send. You're probably familiar with most of them, but there are a few of interest. These are Send Using E-Mail, Broadcast Slide Show and Package Presentation for CD.

You'll probably want to email your photo album to family members. That's easy enough and is detailed here. If the photo album isn't too large, email is perfect. Often, though, especially if you've added music or video, email simply won't work because of the presentation's file size. (If you find the email is too large to send, over 3 MB perhaps, try to remove music and/or videos or consider the next two options.)

One option for sharing the photo album if it's too large to email is to put it on the Internet. This is called 'broadcasting'; it's free and anyone can do it. To broadcast a show, all you have to do is click Broadcast Slide Show (from the File tab), follow the prompts (which will require you to input a free, Windows Live ID) and then send the link to anyone you think would like to view it. When you broadcast a show, it's available on the internet *only to the people you choose* and it's secure. To view it, people will have to have the link to it, which looks something like this:

Email the Photo Album

1 Click File, then click Save & Send.

2 Click Send Using E-mail.

3 Click Send as Attachment.

4 Verify the attachment is less than 2–3 MB, noting anything offered in KB is OK.

5 Complete the email and send it.

Important

Share the link with others first, informing them of the time(s) you'll broadcast the show. At the designated time, click Start Slide Show. Don't close this box, though, or you'll have to get a new link and share it again.

Did you know?

Many email providers allow you to send emails up to 10 MB in size. However, they will take a long time to send and a long time to receive. Stick to the 2–3 MB rule for best results.

Another option, Package Presentation for CD, lets you easily create a CD that others can watch on their own computers. This is quite a nice option, first because it automatically links or embeds the required files, including videos, sounds and fonts, and second because it includes the required Microsoft PowerPoint Viewer to play them. If you know someone who would appreciate a copy of your photo album and you aren't sure whether or not they have PowerPoint or the ability to get

Present and share the album (cont.)

the viewer, this is optimal. In fact, even if you know they have PowerPoint it's a great option! It also offers a nice way to create a backup of your photo album, too, in case something happens to your computer.

Send the presentation on a CD

1. Click File.

2. Click Save & Send.

3. Insert a writeable CD into the CD drive.

4. Click Package Presentation for CD.

5. Click Package for CD.

6. Name the CD.

7. Click Copy to CD.

8. Click Yes.

9. Follow any other prompts to create the CD.

Share, present and print

Introduction

You can share your presentations in lots of ways, and the beauty of PowerPoint is that there are so many ways to share! As you already know, you can create a photo album and play it as a photo slideshow for your own personal enjoyment, or opt to broadcast the show over the Internet or send it to others on a CD. You can present any slideshow to any size of crowd at your own pace and change slides when you deem necessary, or you can run a presentation in a loop at a kiosk at a pace you set. You can even email the presentation, provided it's not too large. Of course, there's always more to learn and additional ways to share, and in this chapter we'll focus on several of them: reviewing your presentation prior to showing it, displaying the presentation when you're ready, using presentation tools and printing the presentation and/or presentation handouts.

What you'll do

Review your presentation

Display a presentation

Use presentation tools

Print copies of a presentation

Review your presentation

You can easily preview a slideshow before presenting it. This will enable you to verify the slides are in the correct order and give you a feel for how the presentation will go. If you plan to practise your presentation, you'll want to remember to stop for a few seconds where you expect people to laugh or comment, or stop longer if you think your audience members will ask questions. Beyond practising and previewing, though, you can also run a quick spell check, translate words or phrases into a different language, or perform minor editing as warranted.

Let's start by running the spell check feature. Although PowerPoint will put a red squiggly line under words that aren't in its dictionary, you can still check for spelling errors manually. It's important to explore this feature because it's available on the Review tab, where other options are present, and it's an easy way to see and review those features as well.

To run a manual spell check, click the Review tab and click Spelling. If any errors are found, you'll have the option to correct them, add them to the dictionary and access additional proofing options (click Options).

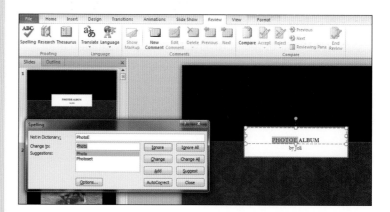

If you're not sure how long a presentation will take to present, while practising use the Rehearse Timings feature. This feature will allow you to monitor how much time you spend on each slide and will give you a total time for the entire presentation; it is available from the Slide Show tab, shown here. Beyond that, though, PowerPoint can apply the timings to the slides to have them change automatically, so you don't have to click to change the slides during your presentation, as you already know. However, if you expect your audience to participate, you may not want to go down this route.

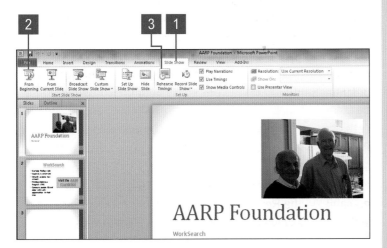

Timesaver tip

You can make edits as desired and click the Save icon to apply them to the presentation.

Review your presentation

1. With a presentation open, click the Slide Show tab.

2. Click From Beginning.

3. If you have not set up timings so that the slides change automatically, click Rehearse Timings.

4. If you have not set up timings so that the slides change automatically, click the mouse once to move to the next slide in the Slide Show.

5. Click Esc to exit the slideshow.

Display a presentation

Transfer your presentation

To transfer the presentation on your computer to another:

1 Insert the USB drive into a USB slot on your computer.

2 In PowerPoint, click the File tab and click Save As.

3 Browse to the location of the USB drive, generally in the Computer window.

4 Click the drive and click Save.

5 At the presenting computer, insert the USB drive and locate the presentation.

6 Double-click it to play it.

Basically, displaying a presentation is just the same as reviewing it (less using Rehearse Timings). You click the Slide Show tab, click From Beginning and present the show. However, chances are good that you aren't giving the presentation in the place where you created it; you're probably going to present at a convention, town hall, community centre or meeting room, and not in your home office. This complicates things a little, because you have to get your presentation to the event area, make sure the computer you'll be using is capable of playing the presentation, and change the resolution of the presentation to suit the available computer hardware and monitor, if applicable.

If you're planning on taking your presentation with you on a laptop you own, and perhaps connecting it to a projector, you won't have to do all of these things, though. You likely already know it'll play on your laptop, the presentation is available on it, and all you have to worry about is making the physical connection to the projector. If you aren't going in this direction, though, you have a few more things to do.

The first thing you have to do is get the presentation from your computer to the one you'll be presenting with. The best way to do that is by saving the presentation to a USB flash drive.

If the presentation won't work on the computer you wish to present on, because you do not have PowerPoint installed on it, you'll have to download and install the free PowerPoint Viewer. You can obtain this software from www.microsoft. com/downloads. With the free PowerPoint viewer you can view, print and open password-protected files created in PowerPoint 97 and later. However, make sure to download the PowerPoint viewer from Microsoft, not a third-party site, just for safety's sake.

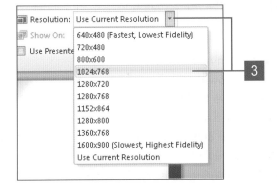

Did you know?

A lower resolution offers a faster response from the computer (or faster transmission over the Internet), but the video quality is poorer than it would be with a higher resolution. A higher resolution causes a slower response from the computer (and a slower transmission time), but offers greater video quality. You'll have to decide what's best for you.

For your information

By default the 'current resolution' set on your computer monitor is used and is often the best choice.

Display a presentation (cont.)

17

Display your presentation

1. If applicable, connect your laptop or computer to an external monitor.

2. Click the Slide Show tab.

3. Click the arrow next to Resolution and choose the appropriate resolution.

4. From the Slide Show tab, click From Beginning.

5. If the resolution isn't what you want, click Esc and repeat these steps to change it.

Use presentation tools

Media controls appear when you move your mouse over audio or video clips embedded in your presentation. For the most part, you'll use Play and Pause/Stop when working with embedded video.

Use presentation tools

1 Start a Slide Show presentation.

2 Right-click the screen during the presentation to see the options shown here.

3 Click Pointer Options and then click Pen or Highlighter.

4 Draw on the slide.

5 Right-click again and select Screen and Black screen.

6 Right-click and select Screen and Unblack screen.

7 Continue experimenting as desired.

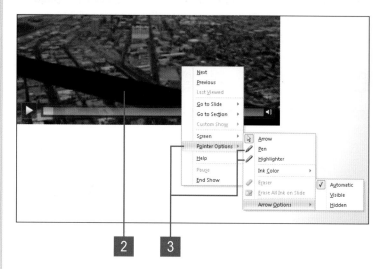

Additionally, during your presentation you can right-click the screen to access other presentation controls such as highlighters, pointers, pens and the like, which you can use to 'write' on any slide in the presentation while giving it. These are called 'annotations', and when you're finished presenting, you have the option to save or discard what you've written. Most presenters use these tools to circle or highlight important data. You can also use the tools to move to the previous slide, next slide, show a white or black screen, and more.

For your information

Use a black screen (or a white one) when you want to talk without any distractions (to hide the presentation temporarily).

As with any Office program, you can print what you've created. You'll also have access to some familiar tools such as Print Preview and Printer Properties. As you'd expect, though, you'll have PowerPoint-specific print options, such as the option to print all of the slides or only some of them, to print full page slides, Notes pages, Outline, or a specific number of slides per page, perhaps two, three, four or five.

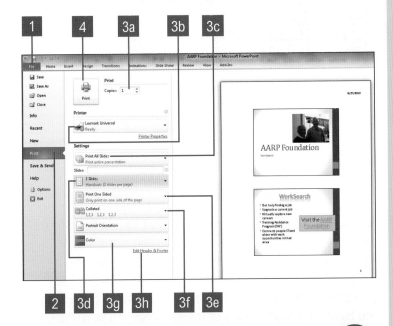

Print copies of your presentation

17

1 Click the File tab.

2 Click Print.

3 Make the following decisions:

  a Number of copies.

  b Which printer to use – if more than one is available.

  c What slides to print.

  d How many slides to print per page.

  e To print on one side of the page or both (if your printer offers this feature).

  f To collate the copies if more than one copy is printed.

  g To print in colour or black and white.

  h To add a header or footer.

4 Click Print.

For your information

Print Preview enables you to see how your presentation print out will look prior to printing. You can use this information to edit your presentation, choose a specific paper or size, collate, print in colour and more.

Important

Click Printer Properties to access additional features such as paper type, paper tray, print quality and watermarks as applicable to your printer.

Print copies of a presentation (cont.)

Print handouts

1 Click the File tab, and click Print.

2 Under Settings, click the arrow that appears under the Slides window, in the area where you define the print layout.

3 Click Notes Pages.

4. Configure print settings and click Print.

You can print handouts for you or your audience that includes your own personal notes, if desired. If you recall, there's an area to write notes when creating your presentation under each slide you create. Handing out notes pages can help your audience understand and keep up with what you're saying, and having notes pages for yourself can help you stay focused while giving the presentation.

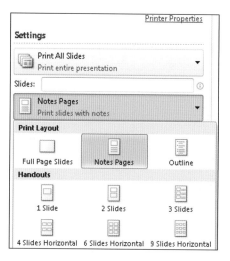

Important

An audience usually appreciates handouts because it gives them your notes and a place to write their own.

Jargon buster

Align – to position selected text on the page. There are four options:

Align Text Left – this setting is the default. Text is positioned to the left of the page.

Centre – this setting positions the text in the centre of the line.

Align Text Right – this setting positions the text to the far right of the page. As you type, the text moves to the left (from the right).

Justify – this setting aligns text to both the left and the right margins, adding extra space as necessary to keep the text aligned.

Animation – a digital, visual enhancement to a single slide in a PowerPoint presentation. Animations enable you to have text boxes, bullets, numbered lists, pictures, clip art and such to fade in, fly in, float in and wipe in, among other things, and you can configure the 'trigger' that causes this to happen, such as a mouse click.

Attachment – a file, picture, song, video or something else that's attached to an email. An attachment has a paper clip icon so it is easily recognisable. While many attachments are safe to preview and open, many are not. Attachments are the cause of almost all of the viruses you'll get via email and Outlook, so you have to be careful.

AutoCorrect – a feature in all Office programs that will automatically correct words that you misspell. You can tweak the dictionary by adding your own words, such as a company name, that it might not recognise.

Blind Carbon Copy (Bcc) – put email addresses in this line to send an email to people who need to see and read the email without letting others know they are included in the recipient list.

Blog – a means of sharing your thoughts with the world (or only specific people) in a type of online diary. Blog is short for Web Log.

Border – generally what's around a picture or page. Borders are like frames, and draw attention to the item or make it appear such that it stands out.

Carbon Copy (CC) – put email addresses here for recipients who should read the email but do not necessarily need to respond to it. Recipients who should respond or for whom the email is intended should appear in the To: line.

Cell – in Excel, cells are the small squares you see in the body of Excel. Cells are, in essence, Excel's 'building blocks'.

Chart – a graphical representation of data. Common charts include Bar, Line and Scatter.

Clip Art – digital (and sometimes cartoon-like) artwork created by artists and shared free via Office.com, purchased on CDs or DVDs, or obtained from third-party subscription services. Clip art can also include video.

Collate – to print all pages of a file at once, and then start again to print the next copy, and the next. If you do not collate copies, the printer will print the desired number of pages for page 1, repeat for page 2, etc. When you collate, the entire document is printed once before printing begins again.

Column – in Excel it's the group of squares that run vertically.

Comma delimited – a text format that can be read by most computer programs. You might export your contacts in Outlook as comma delimited, and then import them in Excel using the same format.

Command groups – each Ribbon tab has commands organised into groups. From Word's Home tab on the Ribbon there are groups named Clipboard, Font, Paragraph, Styles and Editing, for instance.

Conditional formatting – in Excel, this lets you apply highlighting and colour to data that meets specific requirements you set, such as data that is greater or less than a specific amount, is between two numbers or has text that contains specific words.

Contact group – to add members you select to a group you name, in Outlook. This enables you to easily manage the group and send group emails. For instance, if you're producing a theatre production, you can create a group that contains all of your cast members and stage hands.

Contact list – your Contact list contains all of the people you've added as contacts in Outlook. These contacts may have been acquired from a previous email program, from contacts you keep in a Hotmail account or even contacts from an instant messaging program. Of course, you could have added them manually too.

Copy – to copy text so that you can place it (paste it) somewhere else. The original text remains in place.

Crop – to remove parts of a picture that you do not want to appear on the page.

Cut – to remove text so that you can place it (paste it) somewhere else. (To delete text without the option of pasting later, select it and then click Delete on the keyboard.)

Desktop – part of your screen that you see when no programs or windows are open. It's the part of the screen that holds the background image and Desktop icons. You may have shortcuts to your Office programs here.

Document – a file type generally associated with Word. Documents can be created for just about anything, including simple letters or faxes, signs for lost pets or items for sale, family newsletters (complete with pictures), multi-page brochures for a new product or business, or a playbill for a production you're a part of at the local community centre.

Dialogue box – the box that opens when you click a specific command. For instance, in Word, clicking the down-facing arrow in the Font group opens the Font dialogue box.

Drafts folder – in Outlook, the folder that contains emails you're working on and have saved. Generally this is used to hold an email you're working on until you're ready to send it.

Draft view – in Word, this enables you to view the document as a draft to quickly edit text. Some elements, such as headings and footers, will be hidden to make editing easier.

E-Mail – electronic mail.

Files – documents, spreadsheets, pictures, presentations and the like that you create, save, email and can print in any Office program. Files contain your data and are stored on your computer's hard drive. When creating a new file, you can create one that's blank or you can select one that already contains some data by selecting an available template. All new files are created from the File tab of the Ribbon.

Footer – text that appears at the bottom of the page to denote the page number, author, date or other items. Headers and footers, while often only text, can also include graphics, paragraphs and various fields. You can add different headers and footers to odd and even pages, or use a different header or footer for a specific page or section in a document.

Format (text) – this can include making text bold, adding colour or changing the size. Formatting data such as numbers, dates and currency can include changing how the numbers are represented on the page.

Format Painter – to copy formatting and apply it to another part of the document. With the Format Painter you do not have to reapply formatting you've already created in another part of the document or file.

Formula – you use functions to create formulas. A formula created in Excel looks something like this: $=(5*(SUM(A1:A5))/3.2)$.

Function – Excel has its own library of functions, and these functions are grouped into categories. You use functions to create formulas. There are a lot of available function categories, including, but not limited to, Financial, Maths & Trig, Logical and Date & Time.

Header – text that appears at the top of the page to denote the page number, author, date or other items. Headers and footers, while often only text, can also include graphics, paragraphs and various fields. You can add different headers and footers to odd and even pages, or use a different header or footer for a specific page or section in a document.

Host – generally, in web-speak, the entity that offers web space for storing files and a place to save and post to a blog. Hosts offer you server space.

Hyperlink – a way to quickly access a web page on the Internet; you have probably encountered them in emails and while surfing the web. When you click a hyperlink in a slide, your web browser opens and the page is accessed (provided you're online).

Inbox – this is one of several 'folders' in the Navigation pane of Outlook. To access new emails, make sure Inbox is selected. Other folders include Sent Items, Deleted Items, Junk E-Mail and others.

Junk E-Mail – unwanted emails, similar to junk faxes from years past.

Link – short for Hyperlink, a link is something you can click to go directly to a web page.

Macro – a small computer program you generate to create a shortcut for a task you perform frequently. You record a set of commands, save those commands as a macro, and then run that macro when you need to perform the same sets of commands again.

Mail Merge – a feature of Word that enables you to print documents that are similar except for unique elements such as names, addresses, phone numbers, cities, countries, etc. You could use Mail Merge to send the same letter to all of the people in your contact list, while at the same time addressing that letter directly to the intended recipient automatically.

Microsoft Office – a productivity suite of applications. Millions of people all over the world use Microsoft Office to create, manage and edit presentations, data, databases, documents and publications, and to manage their email. It's important to note that Microsoft Office is an application, while Windows XP, Windows Vista and Windows 7 are operating systems.

Mini Toolbar – the small formatting bar that appears when you select text. From here you can quickly apply formatting options such as bold, italic, underline and others.

Navigation pane – the pane in Outlook that holds the folders and offers access to other areas of Outlook, including the Calendar and Contacts. If Outlook looks funny to you, make sure Mail is selected at the bottom of this pane.

OpenDocument – a format used in free and open source programs such as OpenOffice.org and NeoOffice. If you know you'll be sharing a file with someone who uses these programs, save it in this format first.

Outline view – enables you to view the document as an outline and offers easy access to the outlining tools, including expanding or collapsing selected items, and showing only specific levels of headings in the document. (To exit this view, click Close Outline View.)

Paste – to insert text somewhere else that you've previously cut or copied (the same document, a new document, an email, a presentation or just about anywhere).

Photo Album – a feature in PowerPoint that enables you to pull photos from various sources, organise them and create a digital record of them in the form of a presentation.

Portable Documents Format (PDF) – a file format where fonts that are used in the file are 'embedded', unlike fonts used in, say, a Word document sent as an attachment. Additionally, formatting and images are preserved. This means that what you create and send is what the recipient sees. You can think of a PDF as a kind of snapshot of your document or file.

PowerPoint Viewer – you can obtain this software from www.microsoft.com/downloads. With the free PowerPoint viewer you can view, print and open password-protected files created in PowerPoint 97 and later. However, make sure you download the PowerPoint viewer from Microsoft, not a third-party site, just for safety's sake. A person who does not have PowerPoint installed on their computer must have this viewer to open and view the files.

Presentation – the type of file you create in PowerPoint, often used in business to enhance an oral presentation. These can also be slideshows that run in the background while potential viewers do something else. You can create a presentation to run a product demo at a kiosk, or use a presentation to show activity schedules, lunch schedules or agenda information, where applicable.

Print range – what you decide to print when multiple pages are available but you do not want to print all of them. You can print all worksheets in Excel or only active ones, all slides in a PowerPoint presentation or only specific ones, all pages in an email in Outlook or only specific ones, or all pages in a document or only ones you select.

Quick Access toolbar – the small bar located either above or below the Ribbon. It generally has Save, Undo Typing and Redo Typing on it by default. You can add or remove items as desired.

Range – used in Excel, a range is a group or block of cells in a worksheet that have been selected or highlighted. To manipulate multiple cells at one time, you select a 'range' of cells. To select cells you drag your mouse over them.

Reply – an option in Outlook to reply to the sender of the email only, if other email addresses are included in the CC line.

Reply All – an option in Outlook to reply to everyone who received the email from the sender. If there are people in the CC line, they'll get your response. (You won't know if people are in the the BCC line, and no response to them would be sent.)

Ribbon – the group of tabs and their related tab groups that appear at the top of Microsoft Office applications. Click any tab on the Ribbon to see a new set of commands on it.

Row – in Excel, it's the group of cells that run horizontally.

Scroll bars – these appear on the right side of the page or the bottom of it if the entire page will not fit on one screen. What you see

depends on the length of your document, its size and how much 'zoom' you've applied.

Server – in web-speak, a server is a computer that stores files and offers access to them when you need them. Servers are backed up regularly and are secured to keep your data safe.

Slides – the building blocks of any PowerPoint presentation. All presentations have slides. Slides contain text, pictures, bulleted and numbered lists and other elements. Once you've created all of the slides for a presentation you can play it, present it, turn it on and let it loop and more.

Special characters – these are items such as a dollar sign, ampersand, Latin or Greek letters or a copyright symbol. These also include characters related to proofing, such as an em dash, em space, paragraph mark or similar markings.

Spreadsheet – a file you create in Excel. You use it to keep track of data, including mathematical data that applies to investments, retirement and budgets, and also data that applies to your business, such as inventory, costs and outlays. You can perform calculations on any data too. You can easily get an average of a column or row of numbers, add specific data, or even calculate interest on a credit balance.

Start menu – accessed by clicking the Start button or Start orb in the bottom left corner of the screen, in the farthest left position on the Taskbar. From there, Programs or All Programs is accessible. Click Programs or All Programs to view all of the programs installed on your computer, and to locate the Microsoft Office folder and installed applications.

Status bar – a small bar across the bottom of all Office interfaces. Use it to review progress of the current task or its current status.

Style – a preconfigured font, font size, font style, font colour and font attributes that you can use as a title, heading, subtitle or similar feature in a file.

Tab – what runs across the top of the Ribbon that allows access to other commands and Command (or Tab) groups in an application. Common tabs include File, Home and Insert.

Tab delimited – a text format that can be read by most computer programs. You might export your contacts in Outlook as tab delimited and then import them in Excel using the same format.

Tab groups – each Ribbon tab has commands organised into groups. From Word's Home tab on the Ribbon there are groups named Clipboard, Font, Paragraph, Styles and Editing, for instance.

Table – a feature of all Office programs that enables you to organise your data, to format a group of data or to make data easier to manage.

Taskbar – the bar that (almost always) runs across the bottom of the screen of any computer, although it can be moved to the sides or the top. A taskbar can be configured in many ways, including with its icons grouped or ungrouped. When a program is open, the related icon appears here.

Templates – documents, spreadsheets or presentations that come with themes, colours, fonts and font sizes already built-in, applied and configured. All you have to do is highlight the text to change, insert a picture, if desired, and save the resulting file to your computer.

Theme – a group of elements that include background colours, graphics and preconfigured fonts, font sizes and matching font colours.

To-do bar – in Outlook, this pane on the far right offers access to a calendar, appointments and tasks. You can minimise or remove this pane from the View tab.

Transition – in PowerPoint, an element you can add so that one slide dissolves into another, slips in from the left or the right, dissolves in and out, or even pans in.

Web Layout view – in Word, this view enables you to view the document as it would appear on a web page. If you're using Word to create pages for the web, this is a good option.

Windows Live – a group of programs and services available free from Microsoft. A Windows Live Account is a free email address you get from Microsoft for using Windows Live services. You don't have to use the account for anything other than logging in to your desired services, though; you don't have to use it as your primary or even secondary email address, although you can. You do need it to blog from Word, or to save files to the web from Word. It also enables you to create, personalise and manage a small, personal website on the World Wide Web for the purpose of storing, backing up, accessing and sharing documents, music, videos and pictures, as well as staying in touch with others.

Worksheet – a file you create in Excel. You use it to keep track of data, including mathematical data that applies to investments, retirement and budgets, and also data that applies to your business, such as inventory, costs and outlays. You can perform calculations on any data too.

You can easily get an average of a column or row of numbers, add specific data or even calculate interest on a credit balance.

XPS – similar to a PDF file, this option preserves fonts, formatting and images, and cannot be easily edited. It is technically called the XML Paper Specification format. Similar to PDF, it retains formatting, can be read on virtually any computer, and is a 'final' document ready for printing or publishing. This is how you'll send flyers, playbills, brochures and the like to a professional print shop.

Troubleshooting guide

PowerPoint